SPEAKING
HEART
FROM FLICKER TO
FLAME

MOMENTS BEYOND THE VEIL

First Edition

Volume 1

APRIL YARBER

Speaking to the Heart Publishing © 2021

23052 Alicia Pkwy suite H 132
Mission Viejo Calif, 92692

Graphic Book Cover design by Amanda Turney
Edited by April Yarber
Creator, Compiler, Co- Author April Yarber
All Scripture quotations, unless otherwise noted, taken from the HOLY BIBLE: ENGLISH STANDARD VERSION-**ESV** published in 2001 by Crossway, having been
"created by a team of more than 100 leading evangelical scholars and pastors." The (**ESV**) is derived from the 1971 **edition** of the Revised Standard Version (**RSV**) text.

Scripture quotations designated (**WEB**) World English Bible
Scripture quotations designated (**NIV**) are from the HOLY BIBLE: NEW INTERNATIONAL VERSION ® Copyright© 1973, 1978, 1984, 2011 by Biblica. All rights reserved worldwide.
Scripture quotations designated (**NLT**) New Living Translation

Library of Congress Control Number: 2021919250
ISBN: (Paperback) 978-1-7379673-0-9
ISBN: (e-book) 978-1-7379673-1-6

This book *is* filled with Holy Spirit Power.

I pray a special verse over all the
contributors and readers of this book.

In the mighty name of

Jesus

PSALM 91

Amen

DEDICATIONS

*This is a book dedicated to
our Lord Jesus
for whom I write, all for His glory.*

ACKNOWLEDGMENTS

I want to thank all the people who contributed their personal stories, sharing openly with me the experiences they have had with our Lord's Presence— about the times that He has allowed them to glimpse beyond the veil, taking their FAITH from FLICKER TO FLAME. These are the moments that keep our hearts on fire. Thank you for opening up to the world, for sharing your experiences, and showing others how truly awesome, mighty, merciful, forgiving, and loving our Lord Jesus Christ is. It is my honor to be able to hear so many beautiful stories of God's love and the impact he makes on people's lives every day in His own mysterious, miraculous, and perfect ways.

As everything is always His timing…

INTRODUCTION

This book is based on many people's true accounts of personal experiences they have had of a spiritual kind.

When I read through the stories, I see a pattern of the Lord showing up in unexpected ways as if to say, "Look my child, I am here. Do not worry, you are not alone. I have been with you all along." It is in these beautiful moments that we feel the wholeness and fullness of God. We feel His Presence and that ever-so calming closeness to Him. As He pulls back the veil, allowing us to momentarily see and feel with a certainty; not found in this world— that we are not alone. It's these moments— just beyond the veil, we know without a doubt that all things will be okay, because He has allowed us to truly see the power of His hand working in and through the situations of our lives, working all things together for our good...

"And we know that for those who love God all things work together for good, for those who are called according to his purpose."
-(Romans 8:28, ESV)

And also, we know that at all times, although we cannot *see* him, He *is here*. We know He sends His angels to watch over us— as He gives to us these beautiful leading breadcrumbs, that take our *Faith* from *Flicker to Flame*, just when we need it the most. We are free to live and move with a refreshed confidence, without the doubts of the world. We are free, yes, to bask in the glow and soak ourselves with the awe and wonder of our *Lord* and His marvelous works.

✝

"For in Him we live and move and have our being; as even some of your own poets have said, 'For we are indeed His offspring.'"
- (Acts 17:28, ESV)

CONTENTS

✝

"Train up a child in the way he should go: and when he is old, he will not depart from it."
-(Proverbs 22:6, KJV)

THE BEGINNING:
ASKING JESUS IN
April Yarber

From the time I was young, I remember having a sense of God around me. I only went to a church a few times when I was a very small child with my grandmother, Hazel. My grandmother was always a strong believer in God, although she did not share Him with the world— not my grandma. She worshipped and praised Him in front of you, so you could see her dedication, but kept Him to herself. I believe I was about 4 or 5 years old when it happened; my first recollection of wanting to stand for God. I had gone with my grandma to church, I can still picture it. The little Baptist church that sat atop a hill which is in a small town called, Rowland Heights, California. I remember I didn't want to sit in the main chapel pews with the big people (the grown-ups). I found it to be boring, so she sent me to Sunday school for the day. I still remember very clearly that time I was there.

The teacher had long pretty nails that she clacked on the back of the book that she was reading to the class. It was a bible story; it was the story of *David and Goliath (HOLY BIBLE.) David was a little boy and was fighting against a giant. If you are not familiar with the story, I urge you to read it. I remember wanting to be David, he was so brave and stood for God. He didn't seem to care that he was putting himself in danger and could possibly be killed by the giant. His focus wasn't on that, his focus was on God. David had such a fierce and awesome trust in God, he just knew that with HIM— *nothing* would be impossible. He didn't wait for the giant to approach, but instead, he faced his fear with courage, and bravely charged forward. He didn't even put on any earthly armor, but the giant was doomed. David had put on the only armor that mattered, he put on the armor of God. David trusted and was passionate about the confidence he had in the Lord, our God. He stepped out in faith in the most fearless way. I remember a feeling that came over me as she read, and for a moment I hoped someday I would get the chance to be brave and stand for God. I felt something as I hoped at that moment, but it quickly slipped away. After the story, she was standing next to me and looked over, and asked if I had asked Jesus into my heart.

　　　She explained to me what it meant to ask Him into your heart. She told me that Jesus loved me so much and that if I asked Him into my heart, He would come and make a home in me, that He would always be with me. So that day I did it, I asked Jesus into my heart. I remember even then, feeling a strong, joyful, emotion. I wanted His love and peace so bad. I think momentarily I remember even sensing His Presence. But that was such a quick glimpse, and I was so young. I didn't quite grasp the whole experience. I know I felt hopeful, I even cried happy tears. But I didn't notice or feel differently for long, not on that day, but later in my life, I would know. As now I have found hope in the days of the past, that at the time seemed so hopeless. At the time, in *that* moment, I couldn't see it; but now I can see so clearly. I can see that God *was* there, He was always there with me. Just as He *is still* with me today. He has been here *all along...*

　　　* *David and Goliath, 1 Samuel 17,*
The Holy Bible.

Many times, in my life I have seen and experienced things not of this world… things with no explanation, things of what seemed at the time just coincidence. The *"what are the odds?"* type situations and experiences. Things of which I have felt and always known in my deepest heart, it is, was, and will always be, God. Nothing to chance, not perhaps, not by accident, no— nothing and no one could orchestrate life just the way the Father, our Savior, the Creator of all, has done and still does today. I will share bits and pieces of what He has done for me and how His plan for me was all predesigned, just like His plans for you. We all have a job, different jobs, but one purpose. His purpose given to us; to love and help spread the Gospel, which is the good news of Jesus Christ to everyone we meet. Hopefully planting good seeds which can lead them to Jesus and to His gift of Salvation…

What does it look like when we acknowledge and experience a spiritual confirmation from God? Well, everyone is a little different.

Do you have any favorite number sequences? I do— mine is 222.

Before I begin, here is something I found interesting. It may mean something or nothing at all, but to me, it was just another way that God let me know that He knew and planned me to write this book; that he chooses the order of the stories, not only for my book, but in our lives. My favorite number for years has been 222. I have no idea why. No rhyme or reason— I've just always felt close to this number, so much so I even wanted to be married on 2/22. So, if I would see it on a license plate or in a phone number, or just anywhere at all, I would get the same feeling I get when I see hearts. I guess I'll call it that "God is close" feeling. Well, for Bill's story I had a few additional questions. So, we were emailing back and forth, and I noticed that in his email was the number 222.

It just so happened that on February 22 (which was coincidental I thought) I sent my uncle an email, and I told him that 222 was my favorite number and asked him why it was in his email. He told me that it was his birthday. I never knew him well enough to even know his birthday, but here I was calling him on his birthday to ask about the number. Needless to say, I got to wish him (for the very first time,) a happy birthday. I really thought it was something.

"HAPPY BIRTHDAY UNCLE BILL!"

Here is how I see it... the fact that I have always loved 222 and that it was Bill's birthday, and his was the first story that I chose for my book, it was a definite confirmation for me. This, as well as every other thing in my life, is all predesigned. This book, I know I am meant to write. So, when you are in doubt, let me reassure you— Gods got a plan, just trust Him. Keep those spiritual eyes open, and in time He will reveal things to you that you may not have seen without your spiritual glasses on. And this we can read in the book of Daniel verse 2:22.

"He reveals deep and hidden things: he knows what lies in darkness, and light dwells in Him."

- (Daniel 2:22, ESV)

Now, we will start with Bill Sterling. Remember, this is my uncle who I never really got to see that much of while I was growing up, so I didn't really get the chance to get to know him. I felt so honored when my mother said that he had a story from his life to share for my book. It was so cool to sit down with him and really see him for the person he is, in just that short amount of time. Even though I do not know him more personally, we are family, and my soul does know his. We are family by more than blood, we are family because of Jesus Christ our Lord, and I know that this is all a part of God's plan, that this was all predesigned. I know in my heart that it is God's will that I got Bill's story, and Uncle Bill agreed.

"They still bear fruit in old age; they are full of sap and evergreen."
-(Psalm 92:14, ESV)

Me, sitting down and talking to Uncle Bill...

     Bill, who is now 82 years old, recalls a time in his life where he felt the presence of something supernatural. But first, he shares a little with me about the present moments of his life. Bill sitting in his chair, back to the window, the sun beaming through. He looks down at his hands... And begins. He starts by telling me about the daily frustrations that he has now, being his age, and with his memory problems setting in. He says, "The worst thing I notice now is my memory... now I can remember what I did in high school, but yesterday is gone. It's aggravating. But then, I look around and I see people with cancer, brain tumors, something that's going to kill them, and I think, don't complain." Bill tells me that he just wants to make it to September. His wedding anniversary is in September, and he will have been married to Marlene for 62 years. I found this to be so touching— as this you could tell was especially important to him. He stopped and paused for a second and added, "At this point in my life I'm not afraid to go.

Somedays I think I really have had enough, but then I think, there are so many people that would change places with me in a heartbeat. So, I say suck it up and move on. Sometimes…" Bill pauses for a moment, "Sometimes, I'm hoping that I can, and everybody I know can, just go in their sleep. What more could you ask for?"

Bill shared with me his idea of dying, "We all have a day, I believe. We just don't know when it is, but we all have a day and when it's your time, it's your time."

And the story begins…

THE SEMI-TRUCK INCIDENT

An Angel Perhaps...

Bill, who was living in West Virginia, had been dating a nice girl named Marlene. After she graduated high school in May, they continued dating for the next few months, and in September they got married. From there, they left for California on a four-day honeymoon. When they arrived in California, Bill had been offered a job driving a 40-foot semi-truck by a neighbor. Now before this, he had only experienced driving a small delivery truck. This semi-truck carried 70-foot-long steel beams. On one trip he recalls that he had a full load and had to travel from what he remembers through the grapevine in California. The grapevine some would say is the entire route of Interstate 5 from Castaic north to the San Joaquin Valley, others say it is only a few steep miles from Fort Tejon to the bottom of the grade.

This is a steep, 5 1/2-mile grade section at the northern end of this pass, so you can imagine what it would be like heading down it for this many miles, in a huge truck with this kind of heavy load on it. For an inexperienced driver, pretty nerve-racking I'm assuming. And according to my uncle, it sounds as if I would be assuming correctly. As Bill was heading down the grade, he could see the steel beams behind him. The ends of them all positioned facing towards the cab like huge steel stakes ready to impale him if anything went wrong. As he descended the truck began to pick up speed. And he thought, "Oh crap!" By this time, the truck was really going too fast to change any course of direction. If he braked too hard, he could lose total control, and those beams could come unhitched— they'd come crashing in, sliding through the rear window of the truck and take him out. He was going too fast, there was nothing he could do, he just had to concentrate on keeping the truck on the road. He said he was 'full of fear.'

As this was happening, he felt a strong Presence in the truck with him. He knew there was someone sitting in the passenger seat, but he was too scared to look over and see who it was. By this time, he was traveling at about 80 miles an hour, or even faster, as the speedometer only went to 80.

He knew he had really made a stupid decision. He thought about the Presence and said, "It could have been the devil saying it was my day to die, or an angel, but I was just too scared to look." As he neared the mid to lower level of the incline, he knew he would have to swerve off to try and slow the truck by using the side of the road. He heard his unknown passenger say, "It will be okay." Just then he did it, he swerved off. Most peculiar, but thankfully— which seemed planned perfect timing— there was a grate of gravel laid out and an uphill slope. A place used to slow trucks, and this one was in just the *right* location at just this *perfect* time. This natural element of the gravel and the uphill climb began to slow the truck. Now his only focus was to regain control of the direction of the truck. He would have just a bit of hope that he wouldn't crash if it responded to him, which by the grace of God it had. As the truck finally slowed, he was able to stop. As he got out of the truck, a couple of passers-by came over to see if he was okay. When he stepped on the ground, he said his legs were shaky, but otherwise he seemed to be okay.

Whether it was God himself or a guardian angel, Bill does not know. What he does know, is that his life was spared that day. He told me it was the strangest thing that ever happened to him and said he wouldn't want to experience anything like that ever again.

April continues…

　　One of my dear friends who is also my co-worker, Diane, had shared a very personal and touching story with me about the unimaginable true journey she went through with her son David when he was just a small child. At the time she had finally shared it with me in the office, several years had passed. But whenever she spoke of that time in her life, her words and her memories still seemed so vivid. Her emotional heartstrings would pull her back there to all those feelings that existed those moments in time, and she would cry. Not only tears of sorrow as she remembered the pain and the fear of the situation, but she cried tears of joy and relief for everything she went through, experienced, and felt. She also cries tears even today, for the joy of being completely grateful to Jesus Christ our Lord, for the wonderful thing he has done for her and her son. I had asked her if she wanted to share their story in this book when I started to write. I wasn't sure if she would, but today she handed me her story in her words. As I read it tears filled my eyes, I couldn't help but feel that much closer to her— my dear friend, my sister in Christ, Diane.

Diane's special verse:

MY REFUGE AND MY FORTRESS-

"He who dwells in the shelter of the most High will abide in the shadow of the Almighty. I will say to the Lord, "My refuge and my fortress, my God, in whom I trust." For He will deliver you from the snare of the fowler and from the deadly pestilence. He will cover you with His pinions, and under His wings you will find refuge; His faithfulness is a shield and buckler. You will not fear the terror of the night, nor the arrow that flies by day, nor the pestilence that stalks in darkness, nor the destruction that wastes at noonday. A thousand may fall at your side, ten thousand at your right hand, but it will not come near you. You will only look with your eyes and see the recompense of the wicked. Because you have made the Lord your dwelling place-the Most High, who is my refuge- no evil shall be allowed to befall you, no plague come near your tent. For he will command his angels concerning you to guard you in all your ways. On their hands they will bear you up, lest you strike your foot against a stone...

You will tread on the lion and the cobra; the
young lion and the serpent you will trample under
foot.
Because he holds fast to me in love, I will deliver
him; I will protect him, because he knows my
name. When he calls to me, I will answer him; I
will be with him in trouble; I will rescue him and
honor him. With long life I will satisfy him and
show him my salvation."
- (Psalm 91, ESV)

Diane's Story...

THE MIRACLE OF DAVID

My son David had always been a happy
and healthy child. He had chubby rosy cheeks; he
was just so cute. One morning I was helping him
get ready for preschool. I said to him "hurry up I
need to change your clothes." I grabbed a nice
shirt from his drawer, tried to put it on him but he
wouldn't let me. He didn't want to wear the shirt I
chose for him. We kept going back and forth about
it. I said, "fine, choose the one you want to wear."
He got a green woody and buzz light year shirt.
He looked so cute in it and off he went to school.

When my son was four years old, he was running around the house when suddenly I couldn't hear him anymore. I yelled, "Where's David?" …I heard the water running from down the hall. I walked towards the sound of the water which led me to the bathroom. Sure enough, I found him in there, where he was playing with the water in the sink. It was filled with bubbly soap. I asked him, "what are you doing?" He turned around and looked at me. To my surprise, his face was full of that soapy foam. I found it hilarious to see him with a huge bubbly beard he made himself. Then a few years later it happened…

The day it came… the dreaded day, it was the worst time in my life. It was the start of our journey through the fire…

One day I came home from work, I sat down next to my son on the couch while we watched a show on the television screen. I had my arm around my son's shoulder when he said to me, "Mom, I have something small on my neck." I said, "What are you talking about? Let me see." I looked at his neck where I saw a tiny lump the size of a pea.

I was dismissive, thinking it was nothing to worry about. Nevertheless, I told him, "I'll call the doctor to make an appointment." I called the doctor's office and a couple of days later brought him in to get it checked out. After meeting with the doctor, he concluded it to be harmless but that he would still like to see him again for a follow-up. By the time my son and I met with his doctor for his follow-up, the lump was a little bigger. This time around, the doctor prescribed my son antibiotics. Despite his effort, the lump continued to get bigger. Eventually, the antibiotics led to a rash. I brought him in again to see his doctor, but he insisted that we continue with the antibiotics. At this point, I grew terribly upset. I told him, "No! The antibiotics are giving him a rash." He was overtly upset with me for stopping the medication.

At this point, it did not matter to me what he thought because my motherly instincts said I need to get to the bottom of this. I needed to know what was happening to my son. Within the next days, several tests were taken, and the results showed everything was normal… until he was sent for a biopsy.

We drove to the doctor's office for the biopsy. I said, "Come on let's go we're going to be late." He got out of the car, saying, "Mom, I can't walk." Confused and worried I told him, "What do you mean?" I rushed to his door and held him up. Most of his weight was on me, he was so weak. We slowly walked into the doctor's office. On top of this, he had a low-grade fever. The nurse in the biopsy room gave him Tylenol for it.

After I witnessed what had just happened, I knew something was not right. A few days later, his primary doctor called me to make me an appointment to see the oncologist. Through all this mess, David had continued to go to school. One day when he came home from school, I noticed he could barely carry his backpack.

I said to him, "What's wrong? Here sit down." I offered him food and water, but he had no appetite. In fact, after I thought about it, I had noticed that he hadn't been really eating anything lately.

We walked into the Oncologists office to see what the results of the biopsy were. The Oncologist said, "We believe your son has some type of cancer, but we don't know what type. We need to wait for more pathology results." He said we could go home, and that we could wait for more results. I said, "NO. I'm not waiting any longer. I will take him to the emergency room; he's not eating or drinking! Someone has got to tell me exactly what's going on." The Doctor said, "Your right, wait here." He came back in the room and said, "We will be admitting your son to the hospital, we have a bed for him." By this time, the lump was the size of a softball. The doctors had to repeat the biopsy for a true final diagnosis, and they were suspicious that it was cancer. The diagnosis came back on 4-25-2010. The Doctor, and a social worker, walked me into an empty room. We all sat down, I was just sad and scared, knowing that it was something bad. He said the words, "Your son has cancer." I started shaking, my arms couldn't stop shaking. In a few days we would have a family meeting, with the doctors, my husband and I would be finding out the final diagnosis.

On the way to the meeting, I grabbed a towel from my son's room knowing that I would probably cry a lot. My husband and I anxiously walked into the meeting. Already, there were some of my close family members, two doctors and a social worker. I couldn't find my sister, we were waiting for her to start, but she had been in the women's restroom crying. The doctors confirmed the cancer diagnosis…

My son David was diagnosed with Nasopharyngeal Carcinoma and Non-Hodgkin's Lymphoma stage 4, at the young age of 10 years old. After the doctor spoke, each time I would cry over and over. He had to wait for me to stop crying, so that he could continue saying what he had to say next. It was the worst pain any human, mother or father could endure. The world was spinning around in my head; it was overwhelming to hear. The pain was overbearing, and I was beyond myself with grief. This was the absolute worst time in my life. I felt like I absolutely couldn't handle this news. It overwhelmed me so much that I felt dead-alive. I couldn't stop crying. I asked the Doctor," Do you think he will make it? Will he live?" …

The Doctor said, "I don't know." The fact that he said he didn't know, gave me a little hope, but deep inside my heart and mind I was devastated...

The following weeks went by, we stayed in the hospital for more than 20 days straight the first time around. The Doctors' explained to David what was happening in a way he could understand. The Doctors' said, "You will need to cut your hair soon because your hair will start to fall out." He had a mohawk hairstyle at the time. A volunteer hairstylist at the hospital cut David's hair short, but not completely shaved like the doctor had asked.
He was so sad after his hair cut; he loved his hair so much. When we came back to the room, he was so upset that he covered his head with the bedsheets. Many days passed by, and no hair was falling out. Thank the Lord, his hair never fell out like the Doctors had said it would. He kept asking the doctors, "When is my hair going to fall, when will it fall, what day?"
The Doctors were not sure why his hair or his eyelashes were not falling out— but they weren't, and thankfully they never did.

When his school friend Eric had come over to visit David, the only way David could communicate at that time was to write on a notepad. Due to his radiation, he had lost his voice for a whole week. He told his best friend Eric in the notebook "Do you want to play video games?" Or he would write to me, "mom can you hand me the controller?" We lived in the hospital for a full year. A Porta-Cath and g-tube were placed in him. I remember when he got out of surgery after his port and g-tube were placed, I waited in the lobby praying and praying, talking to God. The Doctor finally came out and said, "you can come in now, surgery went well." When I walked to his bedside, I kissed his forehead and held his hand and when I peeked to look at his g-tube site, the unimaginable pain and sadness hit me again like a stab in my heart. I felt no one could understand what I was dealing with, the family support was there, but I couldn't stop feeling empty. So later, I realized that God was the only one who truly understood what I was going through.

During that time there living at the hospital, I had heard from some of the other moms, that the same doctor that was treating David had given them a good prognosis for their children with stage 3 cancers. But even some of these children, I would witness die. It was heartbreaking. My hope was fading, but deep within my heart I knew what I had to do, and who I had to go to for help. It was the Lord; He is who I needed to seek and ask for help. The Lord was the only Doctor that would give me hope. And so, I went to Him, to save my sons life. I humbly asked God, "Please heal my son David and save him in the name of Jesus Christ." I prayed tirelessly, I trusted God with my whole heart, mind, and soul, I asked God for His mercy. At the hospital I would sleep next to my son in a recliner chair. The chair was next to a window. One early morning at 6 am, I awoke, I opened my eyes, and the curtains were pulled open, so I was able to look out through the window. When I looked out, I saw a beautiful big palm tree right in front of David's room.

What I saw next that morning, while looking out the window at the palm tree was the most miraculous thing you could ever imagine seeing. I saw an image of Jesus's face manifest in the tree. The palm tree branches clearly formed His face. The shape of His eyebrows, His eyes, nose, mouth, and His hair. I recognized that face, it was the face of our Savoir in the tree. He was even wearing the crown of thorns on His forehead. I stared at the image and couldn't believe my eyes! I thought to myself... "if I just close my eyes for a second it might be gone, but if it is still here when I open them again, it will just have to be real..."

Not believing it would still be there, I did it. I closed my eyes and when I opened them again, it was still there. Jesus' face stood before me like a light of hope. I know now that this was my sign that my son David would live. I stared at it for as long as I could, imprinting it in my memory. Slowly the image began to fade away, but it left me with such peace.

Seeing Jesus gave me more than hope, He gave me peace. I knew that Jesus would save my son. It was a miracle only meant for my eyes to see.

I knew when I told people they might not believe me, so I only shared my experience with my close family. I found comfort knowing that my family would believe me and that this could provide them with hope and comfort as well. From that day forward, I knew in my heart that my son would get well. Sometimes people may see a cloud in the shape of a heart or something they hold dear; this was remarkably similar to that but so vivid and alive. I'm not sure if while you're reading this you will fully understand or believe me, but I wanted to share this truth, sharing the hope that the Lord provided for me during a time I needed Him most. A hope that is available to us all, we just need to believe and be open to receive Him. We all see God winks and experience miracles every day, we just need to open our spiritual eyes and pay close attention. God is always with us, and sometimes He will pull back His perfect veil to reveal Himself to us. God saved my son David's life and now he has been cancer-free for 10 years…

Months after we were told that David was cancer-free, David told me a part of his story that at the time I did not know, but now it makes sense. He said, "Mom, do you remember when my hair didn't fall out?" I said, "Yeah, but why are you bringing that up now?" David whispered to me, "I prayed to God to please not let my hair fall out, not my hair." I was like wow… I told him, "You are funny, but indeed God did listen to you."

After all David's cancer treatments, high doses of radiation, and the chemo treatments were done, the Doctors said that most likely my son David would never be able to have any children. We were given the option of doing a fertility test, but we decided not to. Instead, we decided that we would worry about that later in life. I knew of another child who went through something similar to David, he had done the test and found out that he would never have children. I prayed again, many prayers, asking God to let David be able to have children. Although it wasn't planned and my son is still very young, David has fathered a child. A little girl, who looks a lot like him. Now I have a miracle son and a miracle granddaughter…

My message to you is to seek God, for whatever you need, in whatever you're facing. Jesus Christ is a healer, He is forgiving. He is loving, kind, merciful and miraculous. God is good all the time. I am forever thankful and grateful to God, that through the gift of His Son Jesus, he saved mine.

And an added dedication to my beautiful miracle granddaughter Evangeline,
You are so very loved, love Grandma Diane.

April continues…

The Lord brought me another story to put in my book…

How I met Shirl,

Another weekend was coming, and this weekend, my fiancé James and I were invited to go to his sister's birthday barbeque. He doesn't get to see his sister or his two beautiful nieces a lot because they live out of state. They were here for a short visit to celebrate with the family, so he was looking forward to seeing the girls.

During the week, my babe had noticed he had a rash on his inner thigh that he was feeling a little anxious about. On Friday night we googled rashes, and as many of you know, the worst of the worst showed up on the many possibilities of what it could be. It left James overwhelmed with anxiety. So, Saturday was here, and we got ready to go to the party. After he got ready, he looked at me and said he didn't want to go. He was having anxiety and wanted to see what the rash was. He called his sister and informed her that we wouldn't be coming, but instead, we were going to go to the Doctor's. There was an urgent care that was open just down the street. We went to the urgent care and when the Doctor came in and saw it, she intuitively knew what it was. He had shingles. It wasn't anything to worry about it and was only contagious if someone touched it directly. She gave him medication that would help him get well faster. We decided it was probably a blessing not to be going to the party since there were a lot of little children and babies there. Plus, all the kids, especially his nieces like to climb all over him. So, it probably wouldn't have been the best idea to go.

Since we were all ready to go out and I was a bit hungry, I suggested we go out to eat. Usually, I am more of a homebody, so getting me to go anywhere even to dinner is exceedingly rare. But on this day, I asked him if we could go to a restaurant that I had been to with my bible study ladies a few months earlier. It was a little Mexican restaurant near our home. I can't tell you what made me choose this place, it wasn't a place that I ever decided to go to on my own, but this day it seemed like a good idea to me. So, we decided we would go and if it wasn't crowded, we would eat there. Mind you this was a Saturday night, so I had it in my mind that it was probably going to be crowded and that we would not be eating there.

When we got there, low and behold, it wasn't crowded. We walked in and got seated right away. We were seated in a cute little booth and across from us a little to my left sat a sweet lady and her son. They were enjoying their dinner and engaging in a deep conversation. After we ordered, James and I were talking and suddenly I heard the lady from across the way say something that got my attention. She had said something about the Holy Spirit and how you know when he's leading you or something to that effect. Instantly a feeling came over me— I knew why we were there. I told my Fiancé that I felt like I needed to talk to her. I said, "My Holy Spirit is tugging at my heart, I need to go over there." James looked at me and said, "babe leave them alone." We chuckled and I said to him, "You want me to ignore my Holy Spirit?" Just then I heard the lady mention a time when she felt she had died and experienced a near- death experience. And I looked at James and I said, "That's it, that's confirmation! She's the reason we are here. I'm supposed to get her story for my book. I have to go over there." James agreed as he knew that I was being led by the Holy Spirit.

I bravely got up and walked over to the table. The lady and her son were still involved in what seemed to be a quite deep conversation, so I felt a little intrusive, but I knew that it was important. As I got up to the table, I waited for a second for them to notice me. I said, "Excuse me— my name is April, and I know this may sound a little odd, but I'm writing a book. Well, it actually is my second book, I am a Christian author. The book is a combination of true stories from people who have experienced God in different ways. I was drawn to you, I felt I was led to come talk to you by my Holy Spirit." She introduced herself to me as Shirl, the Book Doctor. In my hearts-mind, I felt like my actions were confirmed once again. As she told me she was a *Christian* book editor, and I was thinking that it was such perfect timing, that I would probably need her services for this book in the future. I explained how I had overheard her speak of the Holy Spirit and how I felt led to her. What I didn't explain was exactly what I had experienced. When she was talking about the Holy Spirit, I heard the word, "Listen," followed by a pull in my spirit, almost like an inner voice that nudged me as it said, "pay attention…"

I knew in my heart that I needed to talk to her, but then I felt a pause of fear momentarily. Again, while I was contemplating going over, I had overheard her say something about her near-death experience and that's when it was *clear*. It was confirmation to me without a doubt, that I needed to get her story for my book. But only if she would be willing to share. She told me she would, and that she had a couple of stories. She gave me her business card, 'The Book Doctor' is what it says, Shirl Thomas, the book editor. When she and her son were ready to leave, they passed by our table to say goodbye. She stood up next to me. We exchanged pleasantries and then she paused, put her hand on my shoulder, looked me in the eyes smiled, "Walk with Jesus" she said. Of course, I thought I knew what she meant, but really I didn't, not until I read her stories. She sent her stories to me shortly thereafter by email, and since she is an editor, I won't change a thing. I will copy and paste her contributions into the book. These are her words…

1.)   A LIGHT OF PEACE

A few years ago, while riding my exercise bike, a strange feeling came over me. And, suddenly, I guess I blacked out because I felt like I'd moved to a completely peaceful place and saw a bright light – kind of like through a tunnel. Then, just as suddenly, I was aware of being back on my bike, and felt disappointed, because I preferred to be back where it was so peaceful. It was probably only a few seconds, but it felt glorious.

2.)   JESUS – MY COMPANION

Many years ago, I went to a Christian Writers' Conference and mingled with many writers, all of different faiths, and creating prose for God. At the time, I was much younger, and walked every morning. Being in Arizona at a gathering made no difference. I awakened early and took my walk.

A young man came walking toward me, obviously taking his morning walk, also. He smiled, raised his hand, and said, "Walk with Jesus" . . .

At that moment in the dry Arizona dirt, a footprint appeared directly in the front of my feet, and I got chills knowing it was our Lord walking with me.

It is absolutely amazing how God works out all the little details of the day, to get us to that right place, at just the right moment…

The way He did to me, arranging all those details just to have me meet Shirl and get her stories.

It's truly fascinating to think about.
Our Lord is just that way. He gets it done; He is truly creative in the ways in which He accomplishes things. Makes sense, as now I am chuckling at myself, (like hello April) He is the *Creator*.

Another divine appointment…

How I met Mason:

I was at work, but something that day with my breathing wasn't feeling right. I couldn't seem to catch my breath, no matter how deep a breath I would take.

I felt like I wasn't getting the oxygen I needed. I felt lightheaded and was afraid I'd pass out. My co-workers, who are like a second family to me, were worried about me too. They told me to go to the emergency room. Usually, I am not one to go to the ER. I would usually go to the urgent care through my primary care doctor's office or do nothing at all and simply just tough it out, but this day I was so afraid. One of my co-workers Fabi asked me if she could take me to the ER, and this time I agreed. I was scared that I might just pass out if I walked by myself. It was so kind that she offered to take me. So, I reluctantly agreed to go with her. I clocked out for the day, and she walked me over to the ER. I felt like I couldn't answer the questions of the admitting staff, so Fabi did it for me, while I sat and waited in the waiting room. After I was all checked in, Fabi went back to work, and every so often the staff would come get me to do tests that were ordered. In between the tests, I would find myself back in the waiting room.

Feeling a little better, I struck up a conversation with a guy who was very nice. His name was Mason. On the second or third time I was placed back in the waiting room, Mason was still there, and I believe we spoke of God. So, he started to share a true story about a time in his life with me. It was about a time he had experienced without knowing it, an angel. That's when it dawned on me, and I knew in my heart as I felt again that familiar internal tug, I was here to get his story for my book. I explained to him that I was writing this book and asked if he wouldn't mind sharing his story in it. He said he would be honored. So, we exchanged phone numbers and I told him I would contact him later for the story…

I had just one more test to do, when my fiancé James had shown up in the waiting room. I introduced him to Mason, and they talked while I went back for my last test. After that I was feeling much better and yes— just as you could have guessed, all the tests were normal, and I was released to go home. On the way home I thought about the way the Lord had gotten me to the ER so I could meet Mason and get his story.

I looked up and smiled. I said, "Thank you Lord for giving me such a beautiful, good purpose, and thank you that nothing is wrong with me, I am okay. Did I really have to go to the ER?" I chuckled to myself and said, "Jesus, I love you."

✝

Today, Mason texted me his story to share these are his words.

Mason's Story...

IN THE ARMS OF AN ANGEL

The year was 1989 and I was living in Newport Beach while attending Orange Coast College. It was between the evening hours of 8 and 9 pm, I had just bought a new motorcycle. I drove up to a four- way stop sign intersection in Newport Beach, around the area where I was living. My friend Kevin was on the back of my motorcycle as my passenger. Suddenly I was struck from behind by a red truck! My friend Kevin and my motorcycle went forward veering to the left and crashed on the street. The red truck went forward veering out to the right eventually skidding to a stop. I saw the whole accident from high up above. All of a sudden, I was back on the ground on my feet. I must have been in shock! I do not know how I was up above and didn't feel anything holding onto me. I should have flown the way my motorcycle and my friend Kevin had, but I didn't...

I watched the whole accident take place from high up above seemingly from a safe distance. When I was back on my feet I started walking over to see if my friend Kevin and the driver of the red truck were ok. A girl ran over to me and was grabbing my shoulder and arm. The girl kept saying over and over,

"OH my God, the ANGEL was so big that lifted you, did you see it? The Angel was so big!" Just then the red truck takes off! Two of my college friends that were on the corner at the time of the accident, jumped in the back of the red truck as it left. They were pounding on the back window of the cab with their hands yelling for him to stop. The driver of the red truck got pulled over and was arrested for drunk driving, hit, and run and endangering the lives of others while speeding

Amazingly, neither Kevin nor I had a scratch on our bodies. Ever since I could remember I've always felt a strong connection and relationship with God. After the angel incident, I had belief without a doubt in my heart and soul of God's divine and Holy intervention.

Always, Mason

"For he will command His angels concerning you to guard you in all your ways."
-(Psalm 91:11, ESV)

April continues…

<u>Divine appointments are beautiful just like butterflies, they appear almost out of nowhere…</u>

Just like when I met Pricilla and Joe, "the Butterfly People."

     I met a beautiful couple a few years ago. From the moment I met them I felt a closeness, almost family-like... Just sitting there, he reminded me so much of my Poor papaw (my grandpa Clarence.) Maybe it was because he was so skinny with big brown eyes, just like my grandpa. There was something so familiar about these two, and I felt a sense of peace around this couple. I do not remember how we started to speak of God, but of course, we did. We spoke of how amazing God is and how HE is so important in our lives. Then they told me that they do something else that is amazing and beautiful— they have an organization to save the Monarch butterflies, and that is where I came up with their nicknames.

They are the "butterfly people." Priscilla, the butterfly lady, and Joe, the butterfly man. And their hearts and spirits are beautiful, just like the monarch butterflies. Sadly, not too long after I met them, Joe had passed away. But my babe and I did get to go to one of their events in Newport Beach, where they let us feed watermelon to the butterflies in a tent with little plastic forks. The butterflies would land on the watermelon, and you could walk around the tent with them carefully, until they would fly off and land elsewhere. Joe and Priscilla educated us on what we could do to help the monarchs. Joe even spoke in front of the crowd about how special the Monarchs are, and he let all these little kids set the monarch butterflies free in the sky to fly along the coast and migrate, it was amazing to watch. Pricilla and I have stayed friends, she is my sister in Christ. I shared with her about this book I am working on, and she said she would love to contribute one of her stories.

I must admit, now every time that I see a monarch butterfly, I think of Joe and of how his spirit is free to fly. I think of how beautiful his love for Pricilla was. I often wonder if God lets our loved ones watch over us, using the birds and butterflies, as if to say, "Hello, I love you, you're not alone. Don't worry there's more, and the best is yet to come." Anyhow, I know there is no sadness on their side of the fence, and it is so comforting for us to think about, isn't it? In those moments that something like this happens— you see a hummingbird, or a butterfly, or just something in nature and think of a dead relative or loved one that has passed on, your soul ties them together. It brings comfort, doesn't it? And at that moment, you feel their peace, which brings you a sense of comfort, and I believe that is why it happens... God allows it. He allows it for us because He loves us. And no good thing does God withhold from us.

"For the LORD God is a sun and shield; the Lord bestows favor and honor. No good thing does He withhold from those who walk upright."
-(Psalm 84:11, ESV)

✝

This day Priscilla emailed me her story, and these are her words...

"This is what the Lord help me to write and even told me when. God is Great All the Time!!"

-Priscilla James "the butterfly lady"

    I have a badge with the words, "<u>Don't Keep the Faith—Spread it</u>." I do not know where I got the badge, or how or when— but I do know why I got it. I have this badge out in sight in my kitchen so that anybody who enters my kitchen can see it. I see it constantly, and whenever I am in my kitchen, my eyes glance in that direction. That is what I just did a few minutes ago, which is why I am writing this today. I want to spread my faith to others for them to feel the love of our God, Jesus, and the Holy Spirit/Ghost in case they have not recognized receiving His loving touch when it was sent to them in their daily walk of life...

Priscilla's story begins...

THE VISION

I will share one of my latest times when I was asked to be strong in my faith. It was a month ago and I was staying at my son's and daughter-in law's home because of the respiratory disease, COVID-19, also known as the Coronavirus. A few days after I went there, my son was told he had been in contact with someone that had been tested for the virus and the test had come back positive.

Immediately, my son went and got tested for the virus and was told he would find out the results in two days. Now the plan set forth for the next two days was for my daughter-in-law and myself to be separated from my son, which we set about to do. I gave him my bedroom, which they had made for me. It had a closed door, and I took the couch in the living room, to sleep on while we waited the two days. During the wee early hours of the second day, I am lying awake, as I usually do because that seems to be my spiritual quiet time— I can hear the best, and I started going over the present situation in my mind.

I started thinking about my daughter-in-law and how we had time these past two days to share our faith. We both had been praying for the results of the test to be negative. And it was so sad, so very sad to not be able to hug or see my son. I didn't even talk to him for the last two days. I could only hear him open the door, to pick up and to receive the plates of food that his wife had cooked and left for him, and then close the door again. I started questioning in my mind laying there, would it even be two days or longer? I knew I had to turn it over to God at this point because He was in control, so praying and talking to our Lord I asked that if it would be His will, that this separation could end quickly and whenever we would be notified, to help us accept the outcome. My thoughts went to how my son might be notified by phone or email and thinking he would come out of the room and tell us, at that point that is when I would know. Then I had a spiritual vision of him coming out of the room going to his wife who had her back to him, he walked over to her, as he reached her putting his arms around her waist and hugging her, and I felt I would be in view to see it happen, I just needed to keep the faith. (As I am writing this my eyes are tearing and can hardly see the words I am putting down on paper, because that is exactly what happened.)

Sometime in the afternoon on the second day of waiting, (March 22, 2020,) I am sitting at the kitchen table. My daughter-in-law is doing something at the sink with her back to the bedroom door (here I go again, tearing.) I didn't hear the door open, but I see my son walk over toward the sink and I'm thinking, 'he can't be in the kitchen.' Then I see him reach for my daughter-in-law's waist, he hugs her, turns her around, and she asks him, "you okay?" and receives his long-awaited hug…

I see this happening and now I know all is okay, so I run over with great excitement, to join in the hugs. We are all hugging, crying, and thanking God! And yes, faith did get us through those two days. I'm just passing it on to all those who believe, to those who do not believe, and to those who might be on the fence of believing. I might add, I was not supposed to be at my son's house. My daughter picked me up to stay at their house to keep me safe from being in contact with anybody that might have the virus, but she found out when she returned to work that someone there had been in contact with someone that had the virus, and she wanted my son-in-law to take me to my son's house before she got home…

Now my daughter-in-law has gone back to her job. I am back in my own home, going about life in my own kitchen, and my eyes again catch sight of this badge with the words,

"DON'T <u>KEEP</u> THE FAITH—SPREAD IT."
And I believe that is how the Holy Spirit works in my life!

In loving memory of Joe, "The Butterfly Man."

And the dust returns to the earth as it was, and the spirit returns to God who gave it.
-(Ecclesiates12:7, ESV)

"Oh, my precious little child, so lost and in so much pain. Shh… listen, open your heart to hear. My plans are not to hurt you or to watch you suffer, but instead, they are for your building up, pruning, and refining, as you are not alone in the fire. I have great plans for you. Oh, why do you let go of my hand and bury your faith under all that is hopeless? I will restore you, if only you will listen, repent, and come follow me."

"And after you have suffered a little while, the God of all grace, who has called you to his eternal glory in Christ, will himself restore, confirm, strengthen, and establish you."
-1 Peter 5:10 ESV (ESV)

April continues…

There was a significantly horrible time in my life when I was a young woman. I drank and did drugs and had been caught in the snare of the enemy. I was naïve and fell into the trap of drinking first, then eventually doing drugs. I was enchanted and deceived by the illusion, that this way of life was normal and fun. I ended up like so many who start off innocently enjoying the party. It drained me and my spirit, and it robbed me. It robbed me of ME and ruined— for a time— many of my relationships. I was so lost. Although I felt

Jesus trying to get my attention, I pushed Him away, trying to separate Him from my life. Trying to hide the person I was and what I was doing, from Him and my loved ones.

My life had never been easy and there are so many things that I cannot bear to talk about, not even to this day— things that are too hard, things that I'm not ready to share, as it is too painful to re-live. During these times, I wasn't even recognizable to myself. I was so angry at God, but He didn't give up on me. Even though I had denounced Him, during one of my drug-induced, self-pitiful, crying fits. He never stopped loving me. He forgave me, just as He forgave Peter in the bible. For those of you that aren't that familiar yet with Peter, he was one of the Lord's closest and dearest followers, but more than that, Peter and Jesus were best friends. Giving into the fear in a situation, Peter had denied even knowing Jesus, not once or twice but three times. And then Peter cried (I'm sure he felt guilt, sadness, and shame) …But what do you think Jesus did? What was his reaction, do you think Jesus forgave Peter? Well yes, he forgave him, Jesus restored Peter. This is just the way the Lord is. He never gives up on his children. He forgives us and gives to us His mercy and grace, waiting for us to admit our wrongs, turn away from our sin, and seek Him.

If He had let me go back then, I would have been lost forever. But He didn't and I'm grateful. He revealed Himself several times, trying to save me, trying to open my eyes, and here was one of those times— that in the moment it was happening I momentarily felt the power, but couldn't truly understand the significance. Although in hindsight, as people rightfully say 20/20 is perfect vision, this time looking back at a bigger view of the picture... well, I can see that it is a clear vision of God's Provision.

I call this—
ANOINTED WITH LOVE.

This is very hard for me to write and share, because of my shame, but I feel it is necessary... so here it goes. One morning early I had been up all-night partying and doing drugs (yikes that feels so horrible to say/write or even think about, but it is the truth and so necessary.) I was in a neighborhood about 20 minutes away from my aunts. At this time, I was homeless. It was before 5 am and I was walking through a neighborhood in Ontario, California.

As I walked, I noticed spray painting and graffiti all over the brick walls which were on both sides of the street, and I briefly thought 'this probably isn't the best area to be walking on foot in.' A lot of the writing was evil. I saw 666 and

demon night and the words, 'evil lives.' Ugly
spray-painted demon faces and horrible images. I
felt a huge amount of anxiety inside, in that
moment I was filled with the fear of evil, and I
always had hated the devil. I prayed in my mind
that no one who could harm me was out here. As I
walked, my heart was nervously beating harder,
and I began walking even faster, picking up my
speed. It was like walking in a nightmare, like
some kind of horror movie. The sky above was
still pretty dark and the air was brisk. Even
though I was walking fast, I felt like I was walking
in slow motion. An array of thoughts filled my
head... Thoughts about the wrong I was doing and
where my life was headed. It was really early
morning, so the sun hadn't fully come out. I was
walking in the quiet before the rest of the world
woke up. Just then I heard something from across
the street and thankfully, it was a lady's voice
calling out to me. "Young girl there, hey young
girl, where are you going? ...You know Gods got
plans for you, you just have to get your priorities
straight. Come over here."

　　　　I don't know why I went to her. Maybe
because she seemed older, which made her more
trustworthy, she seemed so "mother-ish" and in all
honesty, I was scared. There was just something
about her that felt peaceful and safe. I walked up
to her, and she started to tell me that Jesus loved
me. She asked me, "Why are you out and living

this way?" I had no answers for her. She pointed out a necklace I was wearing and told me that it was deceiving and represented evil, she said that I should throw it away. It was a silver necklace and on it a jester, a king's clown, from the medieval days. She said even something as little as this could be influencing me with its negative symbolism. Its symbol was that of a fool, I took it off and handed it to her. She took it and threw it away immediately.

As she went in, I waited outside near her door. She walked into her house and grabbed a bottle of oil. I had never heard of anointing before, and at the time did not really understand its significance. She prayed over me and anointed my head with oil. With her finger, she put a cross on my head with the oil. I felt very strange and overwhelmed with emotion. My tears began to flow, and I began to cry, for a few moments I couldn't stop the tears. Even though I felt the weight of all my shame, I also felt a small sense of hope restored. Maybe things would be alright, but I was still lost inside, and it would be a long while before I straightened out my life. It would be a long crazy journey before I got my "priorities straight."

"But the anointing that you received from him abides in you, and you have no need that anyone should teach you. But as his anointing teaches you about everything, and is true, and is no lie—just as it has taught you, abide in him."
-(1 John 2:27, ESV)

Today I wish I knew the lady's name, and I wonder if she still lives there. I would like to thank her because I know that her words in that moment significantly changed something for me. That anointing I received was something that I now cherish. What it was like in that moment if I could explain it…

It was as if I felt God draw me near to HIM. It was a closeness to God that I can't fully explain. Just in that moment although I was a mess, I had a glimpse of peace, and I knew deep inside that someday it would all be alright. Speaking with the lady— well, it was like truly talking to an angel, which I have wondered maybe she was. All I know is that I will never forget her, or that morning, for all of my life. The morning that I was shown grace and was anointed with God's love.

✝

A LETTER OF ENCOURAGEMENT TO THOSE WHO SUFFER FROM ADDICTION:

To Anyone feeling helpless, (*God* is your *Help*, Seek Him)

To Those who are feeling powerless, (Almighty *God* is All- *Powerful*, Draw near to Him)

To Someone feeling hopeless, (*Jesus* is *Hope*, hold onto Him)

To my Brothers and Sisters, who are having a hard time coping with life, who may be struggling with addiction or any other stronghold. I want you to know, you can and shall overcome this with JESUS. Keep your eyes up and find hope in the Lord. Wrap yourself in His words, which are found within the pages of The Bible, let Him soak you in His love. JESUS loves you! He has forgiven you. All of it, its forgiven. Just surrender and ask Him into your heart, as your Lord. He is your Salvation, and He is your Savior. Ask Him for His strength and to protect you from all temptations. Right now, you may be weak, but He is strong, and He shall help you see your breakthrough. He will break off the strongholds of addictions and the bad habits from your life. Only... will you let him?

For just as surely as the sun will rise tomorrow, no matter how horrible your life may be this day— Hold on I say! For there will come a day… if you do *not* give up when you shall see the beauty in this life that GOD has created and designed just for YOU. You will see it through sober eyes, and you *will* work hard to obtain all that GOD has placed in your HEART and called you to do… and you *will* be FREE. No longer will you be a muted version of yourself, but you will be the true, beautiful you, that God created. You will shine with the vibrant colors of joy and love that the enemy stole away some time ago. You will get them back and shine even brighter than before.

"So if the Son sets you free, you will be free indeed."
-(John 8:36, NIV)

You will be free, and you will experience the love of God— maybe for the first time in your life, you will know what it feels like to truly be loved, and you will understand that you are an amazing creation with a beautifully designed purpose…
GOD, the creator of heaven and earth— CHOSE to create just one of YOU…
You are truly that special to Him.

As always with love, *April*

P.S.
Keep those Eyes up, Hearts open, and Confidence
in the LORD.

> *"And after you have suffered a little while, the*
> *God of all grace, who has called you to His*
> *eternal glory in Christ, will himself restore,*
> *confirm, strengthen, and establish you."*
> *-(1 Peter 5:10, ESV)*

My Aunt Colleen told me that she has a story to share for this book, about a time in her life where the Lord showed up and about the comfort that He can bring. My aunt, when I was younger, was always watching out for me during my early and teenage years. She and my uncle Clay lived across the street from me and my dad, who was a hard worker, and was gone a lot... so they would supervise me when they could. My uncle Clay would always talk to me about the Lord, and my aunt Colleen would hunt me down from places that I shouldn't have been, such as parties. They have helped me in my life so much. Colleen and Clay have so many amazing stories of God's love to share, and here is one of her stories....

✝

"Beside them the birds of the heavens dwell;
they sing among the branches."
-(Psalm 104:12, ESV)

Colleen's story...

BLUE-BIRD ON MY SHOULDER

I woke up one morning, and I was not able to get out of bed. This was something that I never experienced before... I felt like I was having a heart attack, I was so weak. I was worried and I laid there in bed for a long while. Then something caught my attention, it was the sound of knocking on the window of my room. The noise took my attention away from what I was feeling, I got myself up and out of bed to see what it was. As I got near to my window... there he was, a bluebird looking in at me and chirping as if he had something to say. As I stared at him, I began to feel better. I got up and went into the living room and sat down on my couch. Then I noticed the bluebird had followed me, he flew to the window next to where I was sitting and stayed with me the whole day. Now it has been two years, and my little angel, the bluebird still comes and stays with me. Watching over me and letting me know that I am not alone. I feel like he is a gift from God, that little bird brings me peace, and when I see him, I am comforted. I have never seen a bluebird like this one in all the 14 years I have lived here in my house.

I was having a hard time in my life when I met him. Losing my mom and my dad, really was taking a toll on me both mentally and physically— but along came my little bluebird, and along came my peace. I know this is a gift, as both my mother and father had a love for birds, so what a better way to give me peace than to send my little blue angel to brighten my days. God loves us so much. Our Lord gives us special gifts to help us get through the hard times, and whatever he uses to comfort us in our moments of affliction— well, they are always just what we need. And mine was my little bluebird, and he was just what I needed…

In Loving Memory of my parents— always and forever shining in my heart.

Colleen's favorite verse to share:

"Come to me, all you who are weary and burdened, and I will give you rest. Take my yoke upon you and learn from me, for I am gentle and humble in heart, and you will find rest for your souls. For my yoke is easy and my burden is light."

-*(Matthew 11:28-30, NIV)*

"The LORD says, 'I will guide you along the best pathway for your life. I will advise you and watch over you.'"

-(Psalm 32:8, NLT)

My Uncle Clay wrote:

'Colleen explained the topic of your new book as having something to do with Angels or miracles or great things He has done. If I don't have that exactly correct, please forgive me. I am not sure my story qualifies for any of that but here it is. So, April as you know, I was pretty heavily involved in arm wrestling. I am sure you heard many stories and probably actually may remember some of it. I know you were pretty young. So here goes. I will try not to get too far off track. I hope you find it interesting and hopefully useful for your purposes.'

Clay's story…

GOD ALWAYS MAKES A WAY

So, it is hard to know exactly where to start…

I started arm wrestling with my brothers, friends, and just about anyone who was willing from around ten years old. My dad promoted competition among his sons. I had a brother Cliff a year older than me, a brother Cole a year younger than me, and my oldest brother Calvin was five years my senior. Calvin would bring friends home that I had to try and beat. I have to admit that I liked the attention, and I was full of myself and liked to show off.

I was rebellious and cocky. My father was domineering and abusive at times, but he was also a positive force in my development. I cut school and ran with some troubled kids that could be considered bad influences— I was probably a bad influence on them as well. Needless to say, this led to some bad choices. I did work hard as a kid in the family tree business and grew strong physically. I left home at 16 because of an unwillingness to take the abuse any longer from my father. I went right to work full-time as a shipping clerk in a warehouse. I tried to continue my high schooling part-time but that did not work out so well.

Eventually I got in trouble for growing weed and because it was a first offense, I was allowed to attend some drug counseling classes and not have it go on my permanent record. So, the Counselor facilitating the classes made an impact on me as he complimented me on my athletic ability. During the 3-hour long classes held in a recreation building, there was a recess period. With a park outside and about 20 other guys in the class, we played football with the Counselor. Afterwards he pulled me to the side and asked me, what I was doing 'wasting my *God-given* athletic abilities' on weed, and why was I not 'pursuing a career in professional sports?'

This was one of the first of many wake-up calls for me, I began to look at myself differently from then on. At the time, I had no idea how I could make use of my physical ability other than manual labor. One thing led to another and after a short time, I found myself competing at a high level in arm wrestling. This is how I met Colleen, (my future wife) and your Dad, (Al Raney) and the rest of the Raney family. Things happen fast when you are 19 years old. In a short period of time through some unusual circumstances, I became aware of my need for my salvation, the reality of an all-powerful loving, perfect Heavenly Father. I got married, had a baby daughter, and became a multiple-time World Champion arm wrestler. I met a lot of Christian arm wrestlers. One group of Christian arm wrestlers had a burden for Prison ministry. They asked me and another World Champion arm wrestler (My training partner Virgil Arcerio who is recently passed) if we would like to be involved in putting together some events at Southern California Prisons. We agreed and took an arm-wrestling table and the gospel message to Chino and Terminal Island Prisons. The events were well received, and many prisoners responded! Both to the arm wrestling and to the sharing of the Gospel. They appreciated the opportunity to get beat one after another as they stood in line while we took turns showing them the various techniques.

Somehow, the 700 Club and Pat Robertson heard about what we were doing and invited us to be on the Christian Talk Show. They offered to fly us out there to Virginia Beach, Virginia, and talk about what we were doing. I was a self-employed Tree Maintenance Worker at the time and not making much money but was encouraged to go, so I went. It was a humbling experience. I felt somewhat unworthy of all that expense they were putting out, with the cost of the flight, the hotel, and other costs…

So, the day of the departure, I drove our eight-year-old 72 Pinto station wagon to LAX. I did not quite make it all the way there though, because the car overheated. I had to park it and walk the last couple of miles or so. It was an early Saturday morning flight and it seemed like I was not going to get there in time. I was very disappointed with myself as I had no extra money and no credit cards. I did not have enough money or time to call a cab. I was hoping someone might stop and pick me up as I was jogging down Century Blvd, with my thumb out. I remember there were a lot of shops that were not open because it was about 5:30 AM. As I made my way towards the Airport, I thought it odd that a man wearing a suit was just standing there in the middle of the sidewalk. He looked like a tall, successful, middle-aged businessman and somewhat out of place. We made eye contact as I went past. After a few more steps I looked back to see if maybe he was getting into a car or something— but he was gone and there were no cars parked there. There was however a fifty-dollar bill where he had been standing. I stopped, went back, and picked up the money. I looked around; it was as though he had suddenly vanished. No open shop doors, nothing. I stood there for a few seconds scratching my head looking for anywhere he could possibly have gone. I did not have time to wait around.

As I started back towards the airport, I thought what anyone may have thought, maybe I had just seen an Angel. Maybe God sent me that fifty. My fears of missing the flight left me and somehow, I knew I was going to be on that jet. I did not know how, and time was not on my side for making it on foot, so I began to look for taxicabs. Then all of a sudden, a car pulled up. It was one of the arm-wrestling Christians involved with the prison ministry. He was not going with us, but he said he decided to come see us off at the airport and support what we were doing. I climbed in and away we went. It all happened so fast and with no time to spare. Elijah did not know of my car breaking down, he did not know to look for me walking…

I was a little bit stunned by the turn of events and I can't say for certain what happened there that day. I did get on that flight with two of my Christian arm-wrestling buddies and we were interviewed on the 700 Club. When we got back four days later, Elijah greeted us. Holding up my keys, he said he had put a new water pump and hose in, the car was running fine and in the airport parking lot.

April continues…

Divine appointments can start off one way and become another altogether. It all depends on how God delivers them.

"The natural person does not accept the things of the spirit of God, for they are folly to him, and he is not able to understand them because they are spiritually discerned."

- (1 Corinthians 2:14, ESV)

How I met Jackie:

Well, I haven't actually met her in person yet, just online during meetings we have for an online screenwriters' group that we are both in. Jackie actually started the group. I had been daydreaming a lot about someone picking up one of my stories for a movie, and then one day out of nowhere Jackie decided to start a screenwriter's group by posting something in the *CHS, Called Higher Studios, Facebook group. Of course, I was immediately like, "I'm in." I have been wanting to learn to write a screenplay. So, I thought it would be good to join and learn from the others in the group and develop my own screenplay along the way. So far, we have had more than a few meetings and it is wonderful. These people are absolutely hands-down some of the most beautiful, talented, souls I've ever met.

I am thoroughly convinced that God joined us all together for a reason greater than our own.

I'm also very grateful to Jackie for listening to her Holy Spirit and getting us all together. Below is the email from Jackie, who so graciously said I could use her God winks in the book…

✝

Jackie wrote:
'Yes, I've had a few supernatural experiences, but I think they're more like little winks from God. Anything more would maybe freak me out a bit… LOL (laugh out loud). God knows how to meet us where we're at!'

1.) HE LIVES

Last year— when my brother-in-law was racing me to the hospital after my mother suffered a major cardiac arrest and it would be my last time seeing her, we had to stop at a light at a busy intersection. Something made me turn my head toward the driver's side window. Outside in the next lane, there was a license plate on a red convertible that read "HE LIVES."

2.) THE WHITE FEATHER

During that same week, I asked my mom to give me a sign of a white feather to signify that she can hear me. About a week later while my sister and I were shopping at a clothing store, I happened to pass by a display of Jessica Simpson shoes. On the boxes of shoes was a single white feather. It made perfect sense because my mother wasn't the outdoorsy type so I wouldn't find the feather outdoors (which I thought I would.) She loved shopping for clothes so of course I would find it in a clothing store!

3.)   HE HEARS YOU

The one that most amazes me, is the time I had been seeking God for several months and was beginning to have doubts about whether I was even being heard by him. I had just left a Home Depot and I was in somewhat of a cranky mood because they were out of stock of something I had needed. I was at a stop light. I happened to glance down at the SUV in front of me. The license plate read "HI JACKIE." I kid you not.

I don't know what it is about me, but I've always had this insatiable desire to know hidden knowledge, messages and meanings. I know there's a lot more out there than meets the eye and I think God has been unveiling many things for us today that have been hidden for so long.

Jackie continues…

QUESTION:
Are you living as your best authentic self? Are you living as the person God says you are and whom he created you to be? Or are you unwittingly living your life based upon a lie? Perhaps it began as an unkind remark heard in childhood— a derogatory opinion about you that was expressed by a mother, father, sibling, teacher, classmate, or relative. Maybe someone else's fears and insecurities were slowly instilled

in you over time from an overprotective yet well-intentioned parent, and you unknowingly assumed this identity by slipping into it, as you would a familiar pair of comfortable old Nikes. What if you've been living your whole life under this false identity and you've been completely oblivious to it?

MY PERSONAL STORY TO SHARE ABOUT BULLYING:

During my junior high and high school years I was the target of bullying. Every unkind word that was said to me, I took to heart and accepted as fact. It got to the point where I eventually began to believe that I wasn't good enough, pretty enough, or worthy enough. Those years were supposed to be my time to shine. I was an honor student, I excelled in art and sports. I was like a sunflower ready to burst open and blossom. But instead, I shrunk back. Closed my petals and dimmed my own light so that I would in essence become invisible. Because when you're invisible, you no longer can be seen as an easy target. You're no longer seen at all. You just want to fade into the background and disappear.

As I entered adulthood, I thought I had moved past it. But every so often there were moments that triggered emotions of profound sadness. I was the walking wounded without any visible signs of my injury. I felt I was unlovable. How could anyone love and accept me when I didn't even love and accept myself? I actually hated myself and often wondered, what is wrong with me? Why did I always feel like an outsider? A misfit? I knew I was intelligent and talented but why was life such a constant battle to feel comfortable in my own skin? A struggle to fit in— I just wanted to be ordinary like everyone else.

Friendships came and went. Romantic relationships came and went. I was unconsciously self-sabotaging my relationships out of fear of being rejected again. I built a wall of protection around my heart and kept people at arm's length, so that no one could get too close and discover the "real me." But that "me" wasn't the real me at all anyway! It was a false identity I unknowingly assumed, by accepting everything negative that other people said about me. I experienced a few dark nights of the soul. Many times, I thought I was down for the count. Yet despite it all, I never gave up. There was something deep within me that would not allow me to. No matter how deep and dark the pit was, I would always fight and claw my way back up to the surface again, in search of the light, always the light.

After many years of continued ups and downs, I felt mentally and emotionally exhausted. I had been spinning my wheels looking for my purpose and place in the world, and not getting anywhere. Friends were all on track moving forward with their lives, and I felt like I was still standing at the starter's gate. I finally came to the conclusion that no amount of personal self-development books I had been devouring, no law of attraction courses, no ah-ha moments from Oprah, was going to fix me and completely transform my life. No one. Except Jesus.

In the Fall of 2018, I took a deep breath and repeated the prayer of Salvation in my bedroom. In my pajamas, while listening to *Joyce Meyer reciting it on TV, I made the choice to surrender my life to Christ. SURRENDER. I want you to know how scary this concept is for a lifelong, self-professed control freak. I barely got the word out of my mouth. I've always believed in God, always prayed. But surrendering my life? What exactly does that mean? What does it even look like? Would I have to get all religious now? Read the Bible 24/7 and cancel my subscription to HBO?

I had actually been on the precipice of making this commitment for quite a while before I finally decided to just let go and take a leap of faith. But the truth is, I literally did not see any other option. I wasn't getting any younger. I was tired of running (mainly from myself) I had nowhere left to turn. So, I turned right into the arms of Jesus.

Ironically, and to my utter amazement, it was in my surrendering that I found FREEDOM. It had nothing to do with religion at all. It had everything to do with having a personal and intimate relationship with Jesus. And as I started studying His Word, the negative beliefs I had about myself eventually gave way to accepting what God says about me. According to God, I am...

LOVED

"In all these things we are more than conquerors through him who loved us. For I am convinced that neither death nor life, neither angels nor demons, neither the present nor the future, nor any powers, neither height nor depth, nor anything else in all creation, will be able to separate us from the love of God that is in Christ Jesus our Lord." (Romans 8:37-39, NIV)

ACCEPTED

"The Lord your God is with you, the Mighty Warrior who saves. He will take great delight in you; in his love he will no longer rebuke you, but will rejoice over you with singing." (Zephaniah 3:17, NIV)

WORTHY

"Since you are precious and honored in my sight, and because I love you, I will give people in exchange for you, nations in exchange for your life."(Isaiah 43:4, NIV)

CAPABLE

"But you shall remember the Lord your God, for it is He who is giving you power to make wealth, that He may confirm His covenant which He swore to your fathers, as it is this day." (Deuteronomy 8:18, NIV)

VALUABLE

"Look at the birds of the air; they do not sow or reap or store away in barns, and yet your heavenly Father feeds them. Are you not much more valuable than they?" (Matthew 6:26, NIV)

BLESSED

"Every good gift and every perfect gift is from above, coming down from the Father of lights with whom there is no variation or shadow due to change." (James 1:17, NIV)

ENCOURAGEMENT:

It was in my surrendering that I found acceptance.

It is in your surrender that you will find acceptance.

It was in my surrendering that I found wholeness.

It is in your surrender that you will find wholeness.

It was in my surrendering that I found peace.

It is in your surrender that you will find peace.

It was in my surrendering that I found the real ME.

It is in your surrender that you will DISCOVER the real YOU.
And then you can finally become all God calls you to be.

Blessings,
    Jackie Gebbia

"But do not overlook this one fact, beloved, that with the Lord one day is as a thousand years, and a thousand years as one day."
-(2 Peter 3:8, ESV)

April continues…

WAIT… Just when it's needed… God provides!

Sometimes things take longer than we hope for, and in these times, we are called to be patient. I know it can be unbearably hard sometimes...
To WAIT, to STOP, and to be STILL, but we need to remember— most things in life that are worth anything, require waiting. God's timing is always perfect. There is a song by 'Tom Petty' that sums it up pretty perfectly, and what is it called you ask? Like you can't guess, unless you aren't really a Tom Petty fan— it's called "The Waiting" (Petty, 1981). In one of the main verses he sings, "The waiting is the hardest part." And isn't that true? It absolutely is— the hardest part— and it usually comes after the other hardest part, which typically requires doing something. Like taking a leap of faith….

Hey, but aren't there any easy parts? Thankfully, there are. It happens after the action of finally surrendering whatever we are doing to God, so now, the once impossible, seems to become possible and it even seems to become better than the truth of our own imagined outcomes. It's *easier* when you learn to walk in God's will. It absolutely is easier than not. But another hard part is learning just what His Will looks like for your life. How can you align yourself with His Will? Well, you can start off by asking Him; and pray, my faith family, pray…also be patient. Remember, to us, a day is like a thousand years and a thousand years are like one day to God. So, stay hopeful with faith forward, and do not lose heart. Have patience, knowing God will always fulfill His promises right on time. (His perfect, perfect time.)

"God is not a man, that he might lie, or a son of man, that he might change his mind. Has He not said, and will He not do it? Or has he spoken, and will he not fulfill it?"
-(Numbers 23:19, ESV)

I had put a post out on Facebook several times asking people if they would like to share their true stories/God winks with me, and a whole year went by with no answer to the post. A whole year just flew by, but today I reposted, and someone replied. God knows just *who* to send and *when* to send them. Her name is Shannon, and her story is just what I needed to see.

Also, there has been a verse that has been popping up everywhere I look, it has been staring me in the face for more than a few days now. It is from Proverbs.

> *"A generous person will prosper; whoever refreshes others will be refreshed."*
> *-(Proverbs 11:25, NIV)*

Now I see where the verse fits in, it is completely in the timing because it seems so fitting for Shannon's story.

†

Shannon's story...

GODS GOT YOU COVERED

I worked at a restaurant as a waitress, and regularly earned tips. A lady who was a regular customer asked me, "What would you buy if you got a big tip?" I told her I would buy a new winter coat. That *same* day I got a $60 tip! So, I went out and bought my winter coat. It was already winter and so, so cold.

Sometime later, I was putting my winter coat in the washing machine when my Mom asked me why I was washing it so soon after buying it, I told her I helped someone move and I got it all sweaty. After the wash it smelled nice and clean, it was back to good as new. Later that day I had to go somewhere, it was freezing outside and icy. I didn't like driving when the roads were icy, but I headed out. When I was almost there, I saw a man in a t-shirt standing outside on the side of the road with a sign asking for money. He was jumping up and down just to keep warm, and his face was purple from the cold. I didn't have any money but I wanted to help him, so I handed the winter coat out the window to him. He thanked me and put it on right away. It fit him *perfectly*. When I got home my Dad said he had a Christmas present for me, and he wanted to give it to me early. When I opened it, I couldn't believe my eyes— it was a *winter coat*! He could not have known at all what I had done.

Special dedication from Shannon to her dad…

Her favorite verse to share:

"To the only God, our Savior, through Jesus Christ our Lord, be glory, majesty, dominion, and authority before all time now and forever. Amen."
-(Jude 1:25, ESV)

"He who dwells in the shelter of the Most High will abide in the shadow of the Almighty. I will say to the LORD, "My refuge and my fortress, my God, in whom I trust." For he will deliver you from the snare of the fowler and from the deadly pestilence. He will cover you with his pinions, and under his wings you will find refuge; his faithfulness is a shield and buckler. You will not fear the terror of the night, nor the arrow that flies by day."
-(Psalm 91:1-16, ESV)

April continues...

FAITHFUL IS THE LORD, FEAR NOT...

I believe most of us, if not all of us, have at one time or another experienced fear in the dark. Sometimes we may even experience the opposite of the calm, glowing, light of the Lord. Sometimes we may even feel threatened in our spirit, by something, or someone unseen... it might even be a place that may give us a shiver or a chill, that horrible warning that sets off deep inside us as an unsettling feeling takes over. During these times, hopefully we aren't too afraid to ask God for protection. Thankfully, my friend wasn't too afraid to seek God for help. And God provided what she asked, and in the process, He allowed her a glimpse beyond the veil...

It's amazing to think about, but hard to truly fathom for us humans. Although we know in our hearts that God exists, it seems a bit more difficult to imagine that angels and demons also exist.

They aren't just found in movies, but they are found throughout history, within the pages of the BIBLE and are still found today in personal experiences all over the globe. In fact— from time to time, they are still experienced in this present life. By someone you may know, or perhaps even you. Fanning your faith from flicker to FLAME.

"Of the angels he says, 'He makes his angels winds, and his ministers a flame of fire.'"
-(Hebrews 1:7, ESV)

So, when you hear people speak of angels, just know that they are really HUGE, at least this is what I hear from those who have been blessed enough to have witnessed them up close.

"But the Lord is faithful. He will establish you and guard you against the evil one."
-(2 Thessalonians 3:3, ESV)

✝

Monica's Story…

ANGELS STANDING GUARD

I had prayed for my son because I sensed there was something really EVIL in his room, and I was fearful that something might happen to him while he slept.
So, I had stood in his room and prayed, asking God to send protection for him.

I walked out of the room for only a few seconds when I went back in to check on my son. There in the dimly lit room I saw the most amazing thing— and I froze. What I saw was unbelievable… I saw not one but two ANGELS: one on one side of my son's bed, and another on the other side. One facing the window and the other facing the wall. Their wings were closed and wrapped around their shoulders. When I got closer, I kid you not,
one of them turned his head real slow and looked right at me. I said, "What the heck!! OH MY GOSH!!" I was so frightened because these Angels were FREAKIN' humungous.

> *"The angel of the Lord encamps around those*
> *who fear Him, and delivers them."*
> *-(Psalm 34:7, ESV)*

They were grayish looking… almost like statues with sparkling hair, silver-like beautiful crystals. No gender— broad shoulders, and when his head turned his wings opened a little. I'll never forget what I saw! I got on my knees and cried, thanking God for answering my prayers!! They were amazing! I will never forget it!

"And many who had believed came confessing and telling their deeds."
-(Acts 19:18, NKJV)

ENCOURAGMENT:
We all go through hardships, but we don't have to go it alone! God sent His only begotten Son, to save us from our sins and deliver us into the hands of God. He gives us the opportunity to get to know Jesus through the Gospels— and for the unbelievers, doubters, and scoffers, miracles were performed to show others that Jesus *is* the Messiah. To those who are without family, He lets us know that He is our family. He is our Father: and we are never alone. When we are without— He provides! When we feel unloved— He shows us His love and fills us with joy, but we *must* seek Him *diligently*. Amen.

God Bless you always love,
                    Monica

Answered prayers are wonderful, and most likely, answered completely differently than you had imagined. The prayer itself being answered may be in fact exactly what you asked for, but sometimes the package that it gets delivered in is surprising. But hey, what do you expect when your prayer is for a companion; to find the love of another human being? Don't forget, they have prayers too. And isn't it sweeter still when you find out they are *ready* for your love and that they have also been asking God for you too?

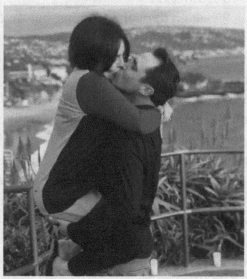

God is so, so, *good*. Believe it and trust Him. His timing is everything…

April's story continues...

ANSWERED PRAYERS

A little more about the miraculous things
God can and does do, is that He most definitely
answers our heart's prayers. I had prayed and
asked God to send me a partner, just like many
ladies do— a perfect guy to call my own, and I
waited for the perfect match to appear. As a single
mom, it seemed like years were flying by. I dated
on and off and must admit, I cried a lot. I was
disappointed even more than that, although I never
stopped hoping. Dating isn't anything I miss. By
the way, my hats off to you single people. I know
first-hand what being single is like, and for most
people it ain't easy (at least not for a single person
who doesn't want to be single.) Someone once
told me (*long ago*) in my prayer life when talking
to God, I should be very specific. So, I took the
time and made a list of relational qualities and
physical attributes that I wanted my dream
husband to possess. I read it aloud to God and put
it away in my desk and forgot all about it. (It was
in there for about 2 years people.)

Then one day I met my husband. After I met James, I accidentally pulled out that list that I had made to God. I was looking for another item in my desk and as I drew my hand back, out came a tattered-looking piece of paper. It fell to the floor so I reached down to pick it up, unfolded it, and a quiet smile of amusement crossed my face. I thought, 'That's odd, should I read it?' The timing was an unspoken hint from God— and I knew as I began reading my description to God, how so ever uncanny it was and is, a perfect description of my now husband, James. God at the time, definitely answered almost all my checks on the list. However, a few of them would be answered later, after James's sobriety. Looking back at the list, (which I have saved for posterity,) it is like I described James flawlessly and perfectly without ever knowing him, but that's just another example of how God works. He answers our prayers in His time and with His beautiful provisions. How grateful we should be always…

OUR FIRST MEETING

I met James during the afternoon on a Sunday near my house, at a place down by the beach, a little rooftop restaurant and bar.

My friend Lauren and I went to have sushi for lunch and then decided to walk over to the rooftop bar to check it out.

As soon as we walked in, I can recall walking right back outside to an empty table on the patio. Walking towards the table, we passed three guys talking to each other. I noticed briefly that one of them in particular was looking our way. I heard him say to his friends, "I want to stand by her." They then began walking over to us and parked themselves next to us at the table. While introducing themselves they added, "Do you mind if we sit here?" I don't know which one did the introduction, I just remember their names, because I found it amusing. Their names are James #1, James #2, and Matt, and I thought it was so funny— the two James. It reminded me of a sitcom I had seen that had 3 brothers named Daryl in it, I still find it funny. Anyways back to my babe, a little while after that, James and I started dating. We had been dating for a few months. We were both drinking a lot, and in fact, he was an alcoholic. I knew in my heart that I didn't want to continue living this way and I thought about my children. Especially my youngest, Autumn. So, every morning on my way to work I would talk to God, asking Him to watch over my children, and my loved ones, and I would always close with an additional prayer:

"Lord, if this isn't the man for me remove him, but if he is, then clean him up, I know you don't want me to be with an alcoholic and that you don't want me to become an alcoholic, so if he is to be

my husband... show me!" I never told James
about that prayer until after God began to move...

WHEN YOU WITNESS GOD MOVING IT IS TRULY AMAZING--

One night my friend Lauren, James, and I
were sitting in my garage and out of nowhere,
James says, "I want to go to rehab." Within 2
days, he called his aunt, and off he went to
Prescott, Arizona. He was gone for 3 months. It
was really hard for me; I was struggling to keep
my faith. I remembered my prayer to the Lord, the
list I'd made about my perfect partner knowing it
was my babe, I saw God moving... but I still
questioned. Over and over many times over those
3 months, I wrestled with the thoughts of unbelief,
not knowing if James would truly come back to
me. I am after all, only human. We all have
doubts— even when we see God working in front
of our eyes. (Oh, ye of little faith.)

During James's 3 months away at the
rehab, another small desire of mine came true.
Because we couldn't talk on the phone, we were
forced to use the age-old way of communication—
writing letters and mailing them by way of the
United States Post Office (also known as snail
mail.) It was a little bit of excitement each time I
went to the mailbox to see if I had received
anything from James, and when I did, it was better

than I had imagined. I had received several beautiful love letters from him, ones just like you see in the movies. It was a fulfillment of a once young girl's fantasies and brought happiness to my heart (and still does.) He wrote some beautiful words to cherish; tangible letters that I could hold onto, look back at, and share with my daughters and grandchildren someday. Anyway, James did come back to me, and we both have been sober for 8 years. When he came back, he had told me a story of something that happened to him... something that confirms to James and to me, that God has everything to do with his successful sobriety. And in our heart of hearts, we *know* that it was the *Lord* who paired us together. He walks with us in the union of our relationship, and the journey of our love. He makes us stronger than we could ever be on our own. We both know that this beautiful life we now have together is undeniably all God, and we thank Him for it. We got married in December, on 12/22. (Remember my favorite number sequence? It's 222.)

My husband James...

Oh, it sounds so wonderful to finally say
that. As I was saying before, he shared with me a
true story of an amazing thing that had happened
to him at the rehab, and he has agreed to share it in
this book. Thank you, honey. I love you...

✝

Shortly after arriving to rehab, James fell
into the routine of his program. They had different
classes and activities to attend all day long— some
of which included AA meetings, yoga, camping,
counseling, and breath-work. If you don't know
what breath-work is, it is a form of meditation
using deep breathing exercises. It was during his
breath-work class where he had the experience.

*"And it is my prayer that your love may abound
more and more, with knowledge and all
discernment."*
-(Philippians 1:9, ESV)

James's Story...

FOCUS ON HIM

I signed up for a breath-work class with one of my roommates at the rehab. He had mentioned to me that he really liked this class and that I should try it, so, I signed up. When I got to the class, we had to lay on the ground with our backs on these pillows that were set up all around us. Then, the instructor started telling us to take large deep breaths in and out. While I was doing the breathing my arms and my mouth tightened up, and I started to go into a dream state. In the distance, I could visibly see my mom, Cathy, who had passed away about a year and a half before this. I wanted so bad to see her clearly. I was trying so hard to focus on her, trying to get her attention, but she wouldn't let me. She kept motioning and directing my attention to the Presence on my left, which was an overwhelming sensation of the Lord's Presence, helping me to realize that He has been with me all along. All the horrible things I had gone through in my life, even all the times I doubted Him, God was *with* me all along.

My mom didn't want me to focus on her. She wanted me to stay focused on the Lord because she knew, He is what I needed to take care of me and get sober. I literally started to bawl like a baby.

I could feel the instructor put her hand on me and all the sudden I was pulled out of the dream state.

The meaning to me is keep *your focus* on *HIM*.

ENCOURAGEMENT:

No matter how alone you feel. He is with you and will never leave your side. And just like my momma pointed out 'He's been with you all along.'…

I felt so lost throughout my life and had no trust in the Lord because of the troubles of my past. I was using my alcoholism to cope, to somehow fill a void. Now looking back through sober eyes, I can finally acknowledge without a doubt that I know God has not only changed my life, but he has _saved_ my life, and was with me through all of it. Today, I am right where I need to be— focused on Him and thankful.

I'm grateful to Him for my sobriety and for the life I live today. I know my momma would be proud of the man I've become.

Special thanks to my momma, for showing me the way!

<u>I love you- Bigger than the Sky Bigger than the Universe.</u>
(BTTSBTTU)
Love,
James

In Loving Memory of James Beautiful Momma
Cathy Hall

"So we fix our eyes not on what is seen, but on what is unseen, since what is seen is temporary, but what is unseen is eternal."
-(2 Corinthians 4:18, NIV)

CONSIDER IT PURE JOY WHEN YOU
SUFFER TRIALS OF MANY KINDS

A journal entry written by April on 3/24/2021...

'Several Days of exhaustion— stuck in the muck and the mire. Knowing deep down if I can just muster up the strength to cry out to the Lord, He would hear me, he'd save me, and help me. I just need some faith.

I'm feeling emotionally drained, bluer than blue. Hopeless, eyes swollen from crying and an emptiness trying to take hold of me. I cling tightly to my Lord, or as tightly as I can. For several days now I have been experiencing the lowest of emotions— lying in bed, crying with a heavy feeling of hopelessness and no known reason behind it... this lowness I haven't experienced for a very long time. I'm feeling so low, almost like a puddle of water seeping deep into the ground. Having worries, yet no energy to worry. Anxiety and nightmares— nightmares of war waged against God's people by evil. A stronghold of the enemy trying to drain the light from within me. I am feeling overwhelmed and weak these days, I have little to no fight left. These times are so hard because you know that He is with you, but you cannot feel His Presence, and He seems so far away...

But my heart knows the truth… He, the Holy Spirit, is here. Just maybe there is something I'm missing— something that I must do, that's why the enemy is throwing his all at me, and this may be why the Lord is allowing it. He is making me slow way down. I'm so puzzled though, as to what I am to do...'

And just a little while later the same day that I wrote the entry above, something happened…

The Lord's timing never ceases to amaze me, just when I am feeling lost and frozen in place, having no words— feeling void of direction— unknowing of what my next steps should be, He awakens my heart. He pulls that flickering faith to full flame, all by His timing of things delivered to me by other believers. He restores us, yes, often times using others to re-kindle the fires of faith and fan the flames. The timing of this story from Joy (which is needed so much right now) couldn't be more perfect. Just as I'm feeling low, crying out to the Lord asking Him what I should be doing, telling Him how hopeless and lost I feel because I don't know what he wants me to do, Joy's story came over via email out of the blue. A ping noise stopped me in my prayers, and I glanced at my iPhone where the notification briefly showed up on my screen, it read *"Having Faith."*

This beautiful, shared God-wink delivered at any other planned or expected time— well, it would lose somehow the spiritual power to push me and encourage me into completing this book....

"And without faith it is impossible to please Him, for whoever would draw near to God must believe that He exists and that He rewards those who seek Him."

-(Matthew 21:22, ESV)

God knows what I need to enable me to keep going. HE knows me full-well, just as He knows you. He knows just what we need and when it is needed most. So now I know, I am to finally going to sit down and finish this book with Faith Forward.

"And Jesus said to him, 'Go your way; your faith has made you well.' And immediately he recovered his sight and followed him on the way."
-(Mark 10:52, ESV)

✝

Joy's story...

HAVING FAITH

On March 7th, 2013, we were headed to
my son's graduation from boot camp. As I shut the
front door, I had an unsettling thought, the same
thought I had over the last few days. I had a
feeling something was going to happen; I didn't
know what it was, just a feeling that I might not be
coming home. I didn't think much about it, as the
thought left my mind as quickly as it came. The
following day, we headed for home, and it wasn't
until I saw our exit sign, I was maybe five minutes
from home, when I had that same unsettling
thought again. I remember thinking I wasn't sure
why I was having these thoughts, as I was too
close to home for something to happen. I was
wrong! As we approached the top of the off-ramp,
we slightly fish tailed. It had rained earlier that
day and the road was slick, it didn't seem to matter
that we were going slow. Our tire barely bumped
the small curb, when my dad, who was with us
said, "Are we going to roll?" The truck rolled
three times before coming to a stop. My husband,
dad, and brother were able to walk away, I wasn't
so lucky.

To make a long story short, I spent ten
hours in surgery, had multiple injuries, and five
blood transfusions. Three days later, I was still
bleeding internally, and little did I know that I was

112

about to take the ride of my life, I didn't know that I was headed back into surgery. I'm sure the doctors thought I was out before they started working on me, but I wasn't. I felt the scalpel going into my leg. I found myself screaming to God for help! I was so busy talking to God. I didn't see Him— nor did I hear Him— but as soon as I mentioned His Son, I found myself sitting on a boat as old as time and I had this feeling of a spirit next to me…

The water was like glass and in front of me, stood Jesus. I only saw him from the waist down; a gown, sandals, and hands— I knew it was Jesus! I thought I had faith, but He said I had little faith and at that moment, I knew that the spirit next to me was Peter. Jesus spoke those same words to him. Our faith is so small compared to Jesus, yet so powerful.

Blessings, *Joy*

"'Come,' he said. Then Peter got down out of the boat, walked on the water and came toward Jesus. But when he saw the wind, he was afraid and ,beginning to sink, cried out, 'Lord save me!' Immediately Jesus reached out His hand and caught him. 'You of little faith,' He said, 'Why did you doubt?'"
-(Matthew 14:29-31, NIV)

April continues...

THE DIVINE APPOINTMENT VIA FACETIME

Even after experiencing all the wondrous
things the Lord has done in my life thus far, and
even after hearing all the amazing true stories
about His Divine interventions, I still get blown
away when I see the map of His provision opening
before me; leading me with an arrow onto a path,
and at its point in front of me stands… His open
door. It's extraordinary the way He has certain
events happen in order to unfold His Divine
appointments, it reminds me that He is Omniscient
and that we are always living in the Presence of
God. That knowing gives me a sense of deep
peace that only He can give and leaves me in
relaxed gratitude. I can surrender my worries,
knowing that everything is in His great hands. (In
these moments I can see it, His Will.) I had
thought I was just about ready to publish and be
done with this book, but God has other plans for
me, and He doesn't hold back. It will be done after
every story He has meant for the book is available
and delivered, right on time. It was a Wednesday,
and I was at work as usual.

I had only been there for about 2 hours
when it was obvious to myself, and my boss, that I
just wasn't feeling right. So, she suggested I

should go to my doctor's and long story short, I am off work for the rest of the month.

I left work early that day and stopped to get an afternoon coffee. I was talking to one of my aunts on the phone when suddenly, my phone went cuckoo, and it began face-timing someone named Agnes. Honestly, it took me a moment before I realized it was this sweet lady named Agnes that I met at a bible study about two years earlier— who, I might add— I had never talked to on the phone before. We only emailed a few times back and forth. I stood outside the coffee shop looking at my phone thinking, 'am I going to bother her, should I hang up?' But I had a feeling there was a reason that this was happening, so I just let it ring, and Agnes answered. There she was, I could see her kind face on my phone. We began laughing as I explained how by accident, (oops, I mean a purpose-driven divine intervention) my phone had butt-dialed/face-timed her, calling her out of the blue. It was so nice to see her...

I told her maybe the Lord wanted me to pray for her, and that's why my phone called. She asked me how I was doing and then I told her that I was finally finishing my second book. She remembered me talking about it at the bible study so very long ago and asked if it was the book of testimonies. I explained it was more like people's true moments where they had very strong encounters with God, like God-winks, stories of angels and other divine-type appointments. Immediately she said, "that's very interesting, I actually have had three very powerful experiences to share in the book." I smiled and looked up. "Isn't that just so Jesus," I said, "I can't make this stuff up!" Agnes and I were both in awe of how Jesus worked out both our schedules so that we could have this divine appointment. She shared her stories with me, and I could see that they were so perfect for this book. All I can say is thank you Lord for your provision.

✝

"Praise the LORD, you His angels, you mighty ones who do his bidding, who obey his word. Praise the LORD, all his heavenly hosts, you his servants who do his will. Praise the LORD, all his works everywhere in his dominion. Praise the LORD, my soul."
-(Psalm 103:20-22, NIV)

1.)   THE EARTH ANGEL

It was in November of 2008; I was on my way to buy some new shoes for my son's wedding in December. When I arrived at the mall, I was going down the stairs to go inside one of the large department stores and misjudged the last step. As I slipped and fell, for a split second it felt as if something or someone lifted me up so that I fell down gently. I fell right by a bench where a woman was sitting. She moved me against the nearby wall and said she was a nurse, and if I would mind if she checked my legs. I felt so fortunate that someone so thoughtful was there to help since I was there alone. She examined my ankles and said she would stay with me until the store manager called the EMTs. When the store manager came out and said an ambulance was on the way; I turned around to tell the nurse thank you and she was gone, just that quick... The fall could have been a lot worse but because of the gentle fall, I broke my left ankle and sprained my right ankle instead of falling on my elbows. I call the nurse that helped me that day, my earth angel.

2.)   THE VISITING ANGEL

Here is my second experience about two weeks after my mom passed away. My mom, Katie, was a sweet, nurturing, and loving mother. She came to live with my husband and I after she suffered a stroke. My mom was with us here in California for seven years before she passed away from an abdominal aneurysm. One day about two weeks after my mom passed, I came home from work and as I parked the car in the driveway a man came up behind me and said, "excuse me, can you tell me where Albatross St. is in the neighborhood?" He had a very strong European accent (my mother was German, and she also had a strong German accent.) That's why I really felt strange, yet I didn't feel frightened. He had this very peaceful demeanor and the bluest eyes I've ever seen. He said he was jogging and didn't know how to get out of the cul-de-sac which I thought strange since he was jogging and had to have come in the neighborhood in some manner. After I told him where I thought the street he was looking for might be, he said, "thanks," and started to head in that direction. I bent down for a few seconds to get my purse out of the car and turned back around to make sure he was heading in the right direction. When I looked up, he was gone. I thought to myself, 'how could he have gotten to the street that fast?' I was so stunned I looked in both directions and then ran into the house to ask my son if he heard me talking to a man (just to confirm what I just experienced) My son said, "yes, I heard him, what did he want?" I told my son that he just wanted to know where a certain street might be because he was lost and didn't know how to find his way out of the neighborhood, but he must have been a very fast jogger because when I turned around only after a few seconds, he had just disappeared.

I feel that experience was my mom's spirit or a visiting angel trying to find their way home, and it was God's way of providing me a sense of peace since my husband and I were in deep mourning from our loss.

Here's the last experience I wanted to share… It happened about 20 years ago when my youngest son got into a little trouble…

3.)   THE ANGEL OF COMFORT

I went to pick my son up from the Huntington Beach civic center courthouse. I was very distraught and saddened by the path my son had taken. As I waited outside for him to be released, a young man about the age of my son came up behind me and said, "Excuse me, I'm sorry for what you're going through, but don't worry everything will be okay." I didn't feel frightened or apprehensive when he asked me to come sit down on a nearby bench. As we sat down, a sense of peace came upon me. The young man said, "I know your pain and your hurt but don't worry, things will work out. Trust me because I've been there." All I could say was, "I sure hope so," and thanked him for being so kind. I was puzzled and I wondered how he knew what I was going through. I never told him about my son being in trouble. As I was looking down, I looked up briefly and saw him get up to walk away, but in a few seconds, he was gone. It was a very strange, yet comforting feeling that I experienced that day, which helped me get through the sadness…

I feel that young man was an angel of comfort, sent by the Lord just when I needed him most.

"And God is able to make all grace abound to you, so having all sufficiency in all things at all times, you may abound in every good work."
-(2 Corinthians 9:8, ESV)

April continues-

HE CALLS US FOR HIS GLORY, TO BE TRANSPARENT AND HONEST— SHARING WITH OTHERS THE JOYS OF OUR EXPERIENCES AND TESTIMONIES, SHOWING THE PURPOSES THAT ARE REVEALED TO US IN HIS DIVINE NATURE, AND WE ARE CALLED ALSO TO SHARE THE THINGS THAT ARE HARD FOR US TO BEAR.

No matter what the circumstance, God will bring something good out of it.

✝

Nicole's stories...

1.)   AWAKENING DESIRE

I have met many people that love Jesus yet say they don't "hear" from God. I would have to back up and tell you how I came to surrendering my life to Jesus. I grew up in an atheist home. My parents were divorced, and my mom was an atheist. I was told my whole life that there was no God or devil, and we just live this life— then get buried and that's it. The night of July 1, 2010, after I had put my kids to bed, I sat on my bedroom floor weeping with my .38 in my hand at the point of just taking my life. The devil was saying things like I'm a terrible mom, all I've done is screw up their lives and everyone would be better off without me. Mind you, it sounded very much like my own thoughts (I know better now.) I'm not sure what it was, I can only assume the Holy Spirit intervened on what I was about to do. I lifted my head and said aloud, "okay God— if you want this life, you can have it, I've done nothing but screw it up." All I know is after that, I was able to get up off the floor and go to bed.

The next morning, I had a burning desire to know this Jesus. I didn't own a bible, nor did I know anything about being a Christian, but I did wake up different and The Lord just started speaking to me. I knew His voice. I think one main reason was that I didn't have any religion in my head to tell me otherwise. I know a lot of people that have had to unlearn and repent of wrong mindsets because of the denomination or the "man rules" that they were taught growing up. I hope this helps and I declare open ears and eyes for you, that you will come into a fullness of "knowing" the Godhead, Father, Son, and Holy Spirit, and that They may direct your every step! In the mighty name of Jesus Amen!!

"My sheep hear my voice, and I know them, and they follow me. I give them eternal life, and they will never perish, and no one is able to snatch them out of my hand. My Father who has given them to me, is greater than all, and no one is able to snatch them out of the Father's hand. I and the Father are one."
-(John 10:27-30, ESV)

2.)   THE FIRST ASSIGNMENT

I thought I would share my first assignment from the Lord. I turned my life over to Jesus on July 10, 2010. My husband and I were separated at the time, and I was only working a small part-time job on the weekend.

No money to speak of and scared to death how I was going to support myself, my 3 kids, and keep homeschooling them. I was driving to the church I was attending at the time, and I missed my freeway exit. I ended up turning around in downtown Houston in a pretty bad area. I was a little panicked trying to figure out how to get to where I needed to be. I was at a stoplight and looked over and saw a group of homeless people hanging out or camped out. The Lord said, "take care of those people." I said, "what?" And He told me again to take care of them. I thought 'what do you mean and how am I going to do that?' One thing I do know how to do, and love doing, is cooking. I made the decision to bring them some food. The next Sunday I made a bunch of breakfast tacos and snacks, got some juice, and put them in individual bags. I drove to the same spot and pulled over to the curb. As if they were waiting for me, two men came over and took the bags from me. I did that for a couple of more weeks and then one morning the Lord said, "I want you to get out."

I was like, 'get out... Get out and do what?' He said, "Just get out and tell them your story." Mind you, I am only a few weeks old in the Lord and know little to nothing about the Bible or anything else other than the voice of the Lord. So, I got out and shared my story, and for a few months took care of those people with a weekly meal, some clothes and a couple of other things. I never gave them any money and they never asked me for any.

The point of the story is that if you want to help people, but you are waiting to get yourself together, you may be doing it *wrong*. Just listen; the Lord will give you someone or several someone's you can start helping now. In the end my husband came to Christ, we reconciled our marriage, the homeless camp got shut down and I never saw that particular group again. I 100% believe helping them was more to get my mind off myself and everything I was going through and focus on those that were way worse off than me. It was the sweetest few months that got me through a horrible time in my life. And this was just the first one, there have been many more!

3.)   A SINGLE ROSE

On Mother's Day weekend back in 2019, I had attended a worship service with my husband, my mom, my two youngest kids, and my three grandchildren. I usually would sit and worship upfront of the church, but today, the Lord had told me to go to the back. I went to the back leaving my family up front and closed my eyes. When I opened my eyes, I saw a vision of my son Joshua standing in front of me, holding a single red rose.

This amazing vision from God was given to me on my first Mother's Day since losing my son.

     I loved seeing my son, but I wondered why a rose, why would he be giving me a rose? I wasn't the kind of lady who ever really liked flowers. Some ladies love flowers, but that wasn't me. So, although I was filled with overwhelming joy seeing my son, I was still a little puzzled. The vision was so beautiful, but it faded away, I wish I could have seen him longer. I went back up to the front and sat down with my husband. After church was over, we were told that another mom and her daughter wanted to do something special for everyone in the church, so we stayed seated. Three dads came out holding their little ones and the kids were holding big heart cutouts. When they flipped them, they each said something on them like, 'my mom' and 'you're so special.' It was so cute to watch, then the older kids came out, all of them holding one single rose.

April continues…

GOD GIVES US COMFORT FROM HEAVEN, ALLOWING US TO SEE HIS MERCIES AND WITH THEM THEY BRING SUCH A DEEP IMPENETRABLE PEACE.

Today is May 03, 2021. This day may not be significant to many people, but to my family it is. I will tell you why shortly…

Today, as I came out of the grocery store and entered my car to go home. I glanced down and I discovered a little red heart-shaped button on the passenger seat of my car. I thought it was odd as I hadn't noticed it before I had gone into the store, but there it was just sitting there on my passenger seat— smiling at me.
Let me back up a bit, and then it seems that I will have to back up even more so that you can get the full scope.

The heart shape itself has a special meaning to me, as I recall beginning to notice them more predominantly a few years back. They began standing out to me more and more frequently in the year 2010. I noticed I began seeing them a lot.

I didn't really understand at first why they would jump out at me. It could be a heart shaped cloud that I noticed, or a leaf, a rock, a puddle of water… or just anything shaped like a heart that stood out to me, as if it was waiting for me to discover it. The more I'd see them the more I began to realize just who was sending them. At first to be honest I felt like my cousin Stacey was saying "Hi" from heaven— but then, that 'God is ever-so close' feeling began to become more prevalent, so whenever I would see them, I knew it to be something special from God. At times He uses them to encourage me like saying, 'you're on the right track.' Sometimes it's just to remind me that I am not alone, and not to give up. Other times I believe He uses them to comfort me. Whatever the case, whatever I'm feeling and whenever I see them, I see an indication of HIS Presence and love strongly around me. I think of these little amazing moments like a secret conversation between HIM and I. Some people call them God-winks, which is such a great description. This day having found the heart button on my seat I felt happy and loved and felt a confirmation that I was right where I needed to be. Looking up briefly I thanked God for my little love message, I then picked it up and studied it for a moment trying to place where it could have come from.

Nothing rang a bell. I tried to think really hard, maybe it fell off some clothing I owned, but it was a red heart button, and I didn't own anything that had a button like that. So, I placed it back in the seat and drove home. After I parked, before I went into my house, I sat in my car awhile and picked up the button again. This time, I seemed to remember something familiar about it— as I turned it over, I noticed dry glue on one side. That's when it hit me, this button was glued on a ribbon that my daughter Amanda had made in honor of my cousin Stacey.

So, this is where I will back up even more. My cousin Stacey was murdered back in May of 1990.

Her murderer had finally been identified by DNA in 2010 (20 years after her murder,) and it was the very year I began noticing hearts.

For all those years not knowing who took Stacey's life, it was so hard, especially in the beginning. My family speculated and struggled, and many parts of our family crumbled, a lot of us fell apart for quite some time…

Thanks to that DNA in 2010, a database had a hit. It matched the killers' (or one of the killers) DNA to some found at the crime scene of my cousin. His name, Alfredo Rolando Prieto, a scary-looking guy. As I looked at his picture in the paper, I remember thinking, 'demon.' He looked soul-less.

He had already been sitting on death row first in California, then transferred to Virginia to stand trial for more homicides, where he was found guilty in those cases too and held there on death row. The murderer actually turned out to be a serial killer. Finally, in 2015 this criminal was to be executed.   As the judicial system, the court protocols, and processes of the expectant execution were taking place, my family— along with the other family members of ALL the other victims— were holding our breaths, dealing with the undue stress of the back and forth of court. There were futile appeals and last-minute attempts trying to stop the execution from happening. Stacey's mother, Gaylan had suggested everyone wear a blue ribbon during this time. So, my amazing, beautiful daughter Amanda had made a box of these pins in support of justice for Stacey. On the lid of the box, it read, 'Grab a Pin for Stacey Lynn.' They were little blue ribbons with a red heart button glued on them. Stacey's favorite color was red. Yes, makes sense, all these memories came flooding back. Just as they are now as I give a thought to them.

Anyway, fast forward to current 2021. I was sitting in my car holding the button, and this time, I remembered where it came from. A reminder of Stacey was with me, and then stranger still was the thought that crossed my mind— 'check the date.' I glanced at my phone and tears began to fall, May 3rd… remember when I said in the beginning that I'd tell you the significance of this date? This is the day that Stacey and her boyfriend Tony came up missing; and two days later on May 5th, their bodies were found. A wave of an unexplainable mixed emotion washed over me. I felt like I was floating out of my own body for a moment. The veil was pulled back and for a moment, I gazed in amazement, a peace knowing Stacey is with Jesus. He was putting her on my heart with love. This heart was to remind me of her…

I don't know how many of you think this way, but I do… I believe God loves us so much that He lets the essence of our loved ones stop in on us from time to time. Not that they need us, but rather, that we need them. I trust our God knows just what we need and when we need it. I also know— no good thing does He withhold from us. Knowing this, I cry tears of relief, but also feel a bit of grief again for the loss of my cousin. I wonder, 'why did the reminder have to be on this day?' This was definitely not a wonderful memory. So, why not allow the little wink, on my cousin's birthday? And then I knew why...

This terrible day of the past connects me with a deeper part of my heart. A part of my heart that is broken and worn (a part that I still *cannot* hide.) It's a place that I hold deep in my heart for my cousin. A part which I believe is necessary at times, in order to fully experience the things that are given us spiritually, connecting our hearts with our spiritual eyes and keeping us from being devoured by the world. Pulling us *closer to God*. It's in these moments where we can feel our faith fanned into *flame*.

It is just what we need— Yes—

A completely vulnerable, wide-open heart, broken down; no walls, allowing us to soak up those amazing, unexpected moments. Pulling us closer to God and allowing us the spiritual clarity, to view the purposes, for which they were intended. Today this little heart-wink gave me the Lord's great peace and allowed me to feel a bit of love from my cousin.

✝

In Loving Memory of my Beautiful Cousin

Stacey Lynn Siegrist

*"So also you have sorrow now, but I will see you
again, and your hearts will rejoice, and no one
will take your joy from you"*
- (John 16:22, ESV)

✝

Darlene's story...

OBEDIENT BLESSINGS

December 11, 2006 - Leading up to this God-wink moment, I had been in a long season of financial difficulties. On this particular morning, the cupboards were bare, and I had no money for groceries. For several days with no foreseeable money coming in, I had been praising God for all my past blessings, and in faith, thanking Him for His financial help not yet received. After my prayer time, God's loving voice spoke to me. He said, "Clean out your refrigerator in faith and prepare it for groceries." So I did. I cleaned the entire refrigerator and even cleaned the kitchen cabinets. With a bit of apprehension, I got ready and drove to our post office to get the mail and sure enough, there was an unexpected reimbursement check for $118.00. Even though I was expecting something, I was still stunned at God's mercy and abundant blessing. I went immediately and bought groceries to put in that clean refrigerator and cabinets.

"Consider this...Whoever offers the sacrifice of thanksgiving glorifies me and prepares his way so that I will show God's salvation to him."
-(Psalm 50:22-23, WEB World English Bible)

ENCOURAGEMENT:

When you find yourself in dire straits wondering how you're ever going to solve your problem— encourage yourself in the Lord. Take a few moments and write down all the positive things in your life. Take time to reflect on how God has helped you in the past, begin thanking Him for all these things, and before long, your faith will increase. You can go to Him with confidence saying, "Thank you, Father, for answering this present need! I give you praise for I know the answer is on its way by faith in Jesus' Powerful Name!"

Blessings,
Darlene

DREAM HOME

I moved to Los Angeles twenty years ago to pursue an acting and writing career. How's that going, you ask? Well, I am a legal secretary by day— writer by night. I've had success and obtained some IMDb credits, but somewhere along the way, I became stuck. Stuck in my day job. Stuck in my dreams. Stuck in my growth. After twenty years I should have been living the dream life in sunny California, right? Let me just say right here and right now, I cried out to God and wasn't getting any clear answers, but what was clear is that my idea of a dream life is not the same as God's. I had a lot of questions. Do I pack up and move home near my family or move somewhere new and exciting and start over again? Can I afford to retire in California? What am I supposed to do, God? I was discouraged, depressed, and felt defeated, but God had a solid infallible plan while I was clueless and crying.

You see, I had been living with a wonderful friend for the past seven years to split expenses. We were so blessed to have our friendship and grow more in Christ during the time we were roommates, which was also part of God's plan!

But I felt like I was just merely existing. I always pictured myself writing amazing scripts in my home office inside my beautiful dream home— someday. The problem— I spent too much time daydreaming and not dream-doing.

We want change but we somehow never voluntarily take action to change things. I felt prompted by God to make a move to a new apartment, but I was still reluctant and nervous about managing my expenses on my own once again and my living situation was working out perfectly as is, so why change it? God was moving me out of my comfort zone because I wouldn't take the initiative myself. And He does that a lot! It was all part of a bigger picture that I didn't see yet. We have to get out of our comfort zones to continue to grow.

In March 2020, I had moved into my new apartment and was feeling more confident that I can do this. Unfortunately, the Coronavirus pandemic had reached a peak and we were quickly given stay-at-home orders. Within the next month, the law firm where I worked began letting employees go and closing down their satellite offices. We eventually took a 10% pay reduction for several months before being reinstated. It was a scary time, but I had to keep reminding myself that God will provide! I held on tight to that in the midst of so much uncertainty. I was so very thankful and grateful to still be employed with a wonderful firm that honestly did the best they could to continue with business as usual (or as close to it as possible.)

I worked from home day-in and day-out with little to no physical contact with others in a scary, ever-changing world. I let the pandemic take over my life and I stopped living it. It threw me for a loop. Too much confusion! No answers! I felt like I had circled back to another mid-life crisis. Everything seemed to come to a screeching halt, especially my writing career and my dream home— not to mention my dream husband, but that's another story God's still writing.

Several months had passed and although it was still weird to keep our distance, wash our hands and wear a mask, it started becoming somewhat normal. And then, one night in November of 2020, I was talking to my friend, and (out of the blue) she mentioned that a home was just listed for sale in her Aunt's community. Why she telling me this when we're in the middle of a pandemic and when I just moved into a new apartment paying a massive amount of rent with a lease to fulfill, I have no idea. I have no funds to purchase a home after taking a pay reduction for close to five months. But after a back-and-forth Negative Nellie on my part, I thought— 'why not look?' Maybe it will give me ideas and inspire me for my future home. I've done it many times before with homes that were way out of my league.

That weekend, I pulled into a very clean and well-kept mobile home community and parked in front of Space 330. I still had my reservations, and this was not the dream home I had pictured in my mind, until I saw the orange tree in the front yard. As I approached the large front porch to meet the realtor, I saw that it was not just one orange tree, but rather, four! And a kumquat tree! Frankly, I really didn't know what kumquats were and had to look them up.

I stepped inside the door to beautiful brand-new flooring, an open dining room with a built-in hutch-type curio cabinet, an open stove area and kitchen bar, laundry room; a guest bath to the side, into a small den, past a second bedroom, and into the back master bedroom and master bath, which a gigantic bathtub and a vanity lit up like a Hollywood dressing room. The master bath alone seemed larger than my storage unit I once had. It was an amazing, beautifully remodeled 1,440 square foot home, with a carport and two storage sheds, lush rose bushes out front, and oh, did I mention the orange trees and kumquat tree? Oh, yes, I did. It didn't compare to my small overpriced 800 square foot apartment where my money was floating down the drain.

But I was still not quite sold on it— just that little hesitation of how in the world could I possibly consider this right now? I was thinking this is nice and someday I'll have my dream home that has a vanity like that, or a laundry room like that, or an open kitchen and bar area like that or— maybe an orange tree, or two, or four! And an extra bedroom to turn into my home office to do all that writing that I'm supposed to be doing because that was my dream after all, right? I just needed a *place* to do it! I was drawn to this. I saw so many possibilities for this home. And then I snapped back to reality.

I spoke to the realtor, "just curious, how much money are we talking?" They had it listed for $129K. That's a bargain for this type of home in southern California, not to mention a safe, quiet, clean neighborhood. My dream home I had in mind was near the half-million mark and stretching further to the million-dollar mark near the beach. But again, my idea of a dream home differs from God's. As I was leaving, the realtor had the duty to remind me that it was a 55+ community and I told him, "I got that covered!" I took it as a compliment.

I left that day with lots of questions and concerns swirling in my head. There's no way I could do this, but it was nice to look. Over the next couple of days, I mulled it over in my brain and prayed so hard. I just couldn't get it out of my head. I was preparing to make an offer just under the asking price when my realtor called and said that someone had already made an offer, so I'd have to go the full asking price. I bit the bullet and did it. Of course, I had to get pre-approved by the bank.

My credit is exceptional these days, but would my income be enough? And then, the down payment? All the expenses of home ownership? Unknown territory all around. I had to close my eyes and hold the rail with each step. I closed my eyes to trust God, not myself. And I grabbed the rail for his steady guidance, not my own path. What was God up to?

Using part of my retirement account was an option. Of course, I would be looking at hefty taxes to pay because I wasn't 59½ yet. But if I look at using my retirement to buy my retirement home, then it made perfect sense and would be paid for by the time I actually retire! I just went with it and prayed— 'whatever happens God, it happens!' I was fine with whatever the outcome.

Then, I received a call from my realtor that there was yet another offer. This was discouraging so I thought of it as a sign that it just wasn't meant to be. My heart was pounding. I was profusely sweating. I just didn't feel comfortable offering more. There's that word, "feel." Quit feeling and start praying! So I prayed. I prayed. I prayed. In that moment I spontaneously opened my Bible to Psalm 131. I *spontaneously* did it, but God *chose* it. I repeated it a few times and what came over me is— things too wonderful for me, content and putting my hope in the Lord now and forevermore.

Psalm 131
1 My heart is not proud, Lord,
my eyes are not haughty;
I do not concern myself with great matters
or things too wonderful for me.
2 But I have calmed and quieted myself,
I am like a weaned child with its mother;
like a weaned child I am content.
3 Israel, put your hope in the Lord
both now and forevermore.

So, I called my realtor and told him that I had prayed and read Psalm 131, and firmly gave him the figure of $131. But he quickly said, "131 what?" My heart sank. More heartbeats and more sweat dripping. I was set on that final 131 until my eyes wandered down the page to Psalm 132:5. My eyes locked in on the number 5, not necessarily the verse, and then I read it...

Psalm 132

1 Lord, remember David
and all his self-denial.
2 He swore an oath to the Lord,
he made a vow to the Mighty One of Jacob:
3 "I will not enter my house
or go to my bed,
4 I will allow no sleep to my eyes
or slumber to my eyelids,
*5 till I find a **place for the Lord**, ...*
***a dwelling** for the **Mighty One of Jacob**."*

A place for the Lord! A dwelling!

You can interpret that any way you want to, but my final response was $131.5, and he quickly said "Congratulations!" The ball was rolling. My mind was reeling. My hands were shaking. My heart was pounding. My eyes were crying. I was sweating. And yet, God was winking!

From that moment on (and honestly way before,) God was in control. He lined up the perfect realtor, the perfect loan officer, the perfect escrow company, the perfect funds, the perfect timing. It was thirty days of my heart racing through this first-time home-buying process in the middle of a pandemic, but I knew this was directly from God. It may not have been the dream home I had in mind, but it was God's dream home for me on this earth, at this time. And my new neighbors also informed me that there were three other bids and one that even offered cash on the spot. But it came down to God saying, "This is Denise's home." Little ole me! He took care of his child and worked out every detail and more when I had no clue. His gifts are perfect.

I moved into my new home on December 14, 2020, just in time to put up my Christmas tree in a bare living room and an airbed in the bedroom. I honored my apartment lease until January 15, one month shy of being there a year and paying the additional month while at the same time making my additional house payment.

But God provided?? Of course, he did! No sweat on his part, but I was sweating profusely as the movers finally placed everything I owned into this new home.

I'm paying less than what I had been paying in rent for a much smaller apartment. I have an investment. I'm in a safe, wonderful neighborhood learning how to take care of the rose bushes, kumquats, and oranges. To come so far from where I was with *no plan*, no hope, and misguided self-direction, God showed up and showed out at a time when I thought it was impossible for me to ever think of buying a home.

So, why didn't I just stay with my roommate until this home was ready? Because moving into my apartment gave me the confidence that I could make it on my own again before He blessed me with such a wonderful gift. Do I worry about the upkeep of my new home? Yes, I'm human, but I know that God will see me through. I'm thankful and blessed beyond measure. He brought me here and He will see me through. God loves me so much! He went ahead of me to lay out the plan and pull me forward to where I was supposed to be. He did all of this behind the scenes when I was crying out to Him for help, for answers— and procrastinating.

I've turned the spare bedroom into my office space where I am writing again and fulfilling the purpose he has for me in this life, as well as working-from-home as a legal secretary because that still pays the bills. God can do anything, and nothing alters his plan. I pray that you never miss out on the God-winks! They're all around us…

ENCOURAGEMENT:

I hope you are encouraged by my story. If anything, know that you *can* dream your biggest dream and place it in God's hands. From there, He will turn it into something much bigger than you ever imagined and you will be amazed by His marvelous plan.

Scripture Share:

"Now to him who is able to do immeasurably more than all we ask or imagine, according to his power that is at work within us, to him be glory in the church and in Christ Jesus throughout all generations, forever and ever! Amen."
-(Ephesians 3:20-21, NIV)

Always in His grip,
Denise

Keith's story...

LAKE SILENCE

It was August of 1973. I had traveled from Houston with a group of 25 Explorer Scouts to Ely, Minnesota for a long canoe trek. Once we arrived in Ely, we flew on "Wilderness Wings Airways," 125 miles into the Canadian forest country and we canoed (and hiked many miles over portage trails carrying the canoes and backpacks) back to the United States. It was a trip of many firsts for me. Among them, it was my first time to travel that far and long without my parents. That flight on Wilderness Wings was also my first time to fly and it was on a pontoon plane at that. We had been on the trail for almost two weeks. We would cross the border back into the United States the next day. It had been a long two weeks. They were a great bunch of guys but over the course of the trip, since we got off the airplanes, I had seen almost no one except for those 25 guys. There are not great numbers of people canoeing through Quetico Provincial Park. We made camp that last night on a little lake about ten miles north of the border. We all went about our camp responsibilities— we pitched the tents, gathered the firewood, made dinner, and cleaned up after the meal. I don't remember, so many years later, what my responsibility was that night. I just know I was finished for the night...

I grabbed my canoe paddle and a lifejacket, threw both into the canoe I shared with two other guys, paddled out to the middle of the lake, and sat there watching the sunset. I knew I would hear all about how I knew better than to go out on the water alone (anyone who has ever had experience with Scouts knows, you don't do anything on the water without a buddy.) I didn't care, I would deal with that later. I was sick of those 24 other guys and needed time alone. I loved the trip, but I had been away from home most of the summer. I had worked all summer in a job that had me away from home during the week but was home on the weekends, and I immediately followed that up with this canoe trip. I was feeling a bit homesick too. Once I was in the middle of the lake, I sat and watched the sunset. There, the lake lived up to its name, "Silence." No, it wasn't completely silent. could still hear the camp off in the distance, but for me it was quiet…

There, in the middle of Lake Silence, for possibly the first time in my life, I felt the presence of God. It wasn't my profession of faith that was a few years before. It wasn't my call to ministry, that was several years away. It was God reminding a tired, homesick teenager that he wasn't alone.

Scripture Share:

"The LORD said, 'Go out and stand at the mountain before the LORD. The LORD is passing by.' A very strong wind tore through the mountains and broke apart the stones before the LORD. But the LORD wasn't in the wind. After the wind, there was an earthquake. But the LORD wasn't in the earthquake. After the earthquake, there was a fire. But the LORD wasn't in the fire. After the fire, there was a sound. Thin. Quiet. When Elijah heard it, he wrapped his face in his coat. He went out and stood at the cave's entrance. A voice came to him and said, 'Why are you here, Elijah?'"
- (1 Kings 19:11-13, CEB)

ENCOURAGEMENT:

We rarely find God in the noise of Life. God is polite and usually will not try to speak over us and the noise we use to fill our ears. It is up to us to seek the time and space where we can hear God speak to us. I used to believe that God was capable of speaking over the noise, and in that much I was right. But God wants us to listen, so God, more often than not, speaks softly.

Filled with His Grace,
Keith

Nolan's story...

(Written 05/25/21)

AN UNDENIABLE MESSAGE

Just a little over a year ago, I was attending one of my best friends' funerals (Brad.) He had recently died from a drug overdose while in his car. In this group of friends, there were 5 of us that were remarkably close. When I returned home two days later from the funeral, I walked through the front doors of the rehab I had been staying at, and the first thing I see is two of the five friends together. One was one of the homies, and the other was Brad's girlfriend. They were sitting on the couch hooking up. Mind you Brad had been in the ground for maybe a day. It really got to me seeing that. So, I grabbed my board and walked straight back out, and skated down to the Santa Monica pier. I was terribly upset at the site I had just seen. I thought to myself, 'Morals and integrity just do not seem to be in people's values anymore.' Once I got down to the pier, I went to my favorite spot, which is a bench at the end of it. I would normally go there to do my meditation and sit with myself when I was upset, it was my safe space. I remember it being a pretty slow day down there, kind of overcast. I was just sitting there thinking about how life is, how people are, and how I wish I had never witnessed what I had just seen.

Once I was about to leave something told me to try to talk to Brad in my head… (I know it sounds so crazy.)

During this time in my life, I was really struggling. I was trying to connect with GOD, however, I decided to try to speak to Brad. I remember just looking up at the sky and thinking "Brad, please let me know if anything is out there, I'm really struggling right now man." No joke, not even half a second after I finished that thought, 25 *dolphins* and *sea otters* started popping up out of the water doing like a little dance in front of me. Not going to lie, I started freaking out a little bit and started looking around to see if anyone else was seeing what was going on. Do I think Brad sent that message to me? I *don't*, I think GOD sent that message to me for Brad, just to let me know that he was safe, and it was God showing himself to me through a simple, yet very cool message. This one girl told me recently that once you let God into your life you will start noticing spiritual messages, things meant just for you. Things you would probably never pay attention to if you hadn't let Him in. And I truly believe that was what He was doing. Showing up and letting me know that I am not alone— *He is here*.

ENCOURAGEMENT:

I have struggled for 30 years trying to connect with God. The thing I have learned is that God might not show Himself today, tomorrow, or even the next day, but *don't give up* because when the time is right, I promise, He *will* show Himself in a way you would never imagine.

- *Nolan*

EPILOGUE

The idea for this book series came to me by Divine inspiration. The stories in it and the order they were written and shared, all appointed by the Lord. He guided my steps every bit of the way. I am eternally grateful to Jesus for such a wonderful and fulfilling purpose. I pray to continue these books— well, until HE says I no longer can.

I hope you have been blessed by these beautiful true experiences, that were so bravely shared. And I pray that you feel that much closer to our beautiful Lord Jesus. Remember no matter what you're going through—

Jesus is with you.
Right there, wherever you are.
You are not alone.
And most importantly;
You are **forgiven** and **loved**, *unconditionally*.

OTHER GOOD WORKS CONTRIBUTORS
PAGE

April Yarber/ Compiler / Contributor/ book-interior designer
FROM FLICKER TO FLAME SERIES DEVELOPER
Speakingtothehearts@gmail.com
Author, _Speaking to the Heart Moments with Jesus- daily devotional_
Trilogy Publishing 2019

Rev. J. Keith Broyles, D.Min./ Contributor
LAKE SILENCE
Pastor, Perritte Memorial United Methodist Church
Nacogdoches, TX
Author, _Average Joe: With an Extraordinary Story_
Amazon Direct Publishing 2019

Jackie Gebbia/ Contributor
HE LIVES,
THE WHITE FEATHER
HE HEARS YOU
Screenwriter, Graphic Designer
Occupy Culture Founder 2021,
occupycultureinfo@gmail.com

Denise Thurman/ Contributor
MY DREAM HOME
Screenwriter, Author, _Heaven won't be Heaven without You_,
Author house 2013

OTHER GOOD WORKS CONTRIBUTORS
PAGE
-continued-

Darlene Harris/ Contributor
OBEDIENT BLESSINGS
Blog Author, *Rooms filled with Treasures*
Website www.roomsfilledwithtreasures.com
Author, Stepping Stone to a Better Life 2018; available on
the website for free downloads

Pricella James Cruz/ Contributor
THE VISION
Co- Founder, *Western Monarch Guardians*
Orange County, California *1998*
Educator, helping to save the Monarch Butterflies
Facebook page: Monarch Guardians

James R Berg/ Contributor
FOCUS ON HIM
Owner Operator, *Crystal Waters Pool, and Spa*
Orange County, California

Amanda Turney/ Cover designer
BOOK COVER GRAPHIC DESIGN
Hair Stylist, Orange County, California

'Speaking to the Heart: from Flicker to Flame Book Series'

Volume 1

Moments beyond the Veil

'Speaking to the Heart: from Flicker to Flame Book Series'

An on-going series of True Faith Experiences…

If you have a true faith story that you would like to contribute for consideration and possible publication in a future volume, please email

at

Speakingtothehearts@gmail.com

-As always with love-
April

✝

NOTES

NOTES

Thank you again, all you beautiful servant hearts who were brave enough to share your stories with the world. Openly gifting to us, your amazing experiences with God and the things of Him– lived in truth and shared in love. Fanning the flicker of FAITH to FLAME by encouraging others by example, to shine their lights BRAVELY. All for Gods Glory...

God bless you all!

As always with love, *April*